Blue Mountains Far Away

GREGORY MCNAMEE

Books by Gregory McNamee:

Nonfiction

Open Range and Parking Lots (with Virgil Hancock)
Grand Canyon Places Names
A Desert Bestiary
In the Presence of Wolves (with Art Wolfe)
Gila: The Life and Death of an American River
The Return of Richard Nixon

Poetry

Inconstant History
Philoktetes: A Verse Translation

Fiction

Christ on the Mount of Olives

Collections

The Mountain World
The Serpent's Tale
A World of Turtles
The Sierra Club Desert Reader
Named in Stone and Sky
Living in Words
Resit Much, Obey Little: Remembering Ed Abbey
        (with James R. Hepworth)

Blue Mountains Far Away

JOURNEYS INTO THE AMERICAN WILDERNESS

GREGORY MCNAMEE

The Lyons Press

Designed by Compset, Inc.

Printed in the United States of America

10 9 8 7 6 5 4 3 2 1

Library of Congress Cataloging-in-Publication Data

McNamee, Gregory.
    Blue mountains far away: journeys into the American wilderness / Gregory McNamee.
        p. cm.
    ISBN 1-58574-014-4 (HC)
    1. Natural History--Southwestern States I. Title.

Qh104.5.S6 M36 2000
508.79--dc21
                                        00-025899

The blue mountain is the father of the white cloud. The white cloud is the child of the blue mountain. All day long they depend on each other, without being dependent on each other. The white cloud is always the white cloud. The blue mountain is always the blue mountain.

—TOZAN

Contents

Introduction

I am not a betting man, nor, at least these days, one especially given to formulating grand abstract theories about the world and its vagaries. Nonetheless, I would put money on this datum as a law of the universe: in the heart of the Greater Southwest, you cannot find a landscape that is not bordered, somewhere, by a blue fringe of mountains.

Those mountains, there on the desert horizon, mean a great deal to me. I have spent the better part of the last three decades wandering in them, banging my knees on quartz rock and keeping an eye out for useful lessons. Without those mountains, my world would be substantially the less. Without them, the desert Southwest, this land on and for which I stand, would be a lesser place—a North Texas with drearier politics. Mountains and deserts are their own argument, and there is no gainsaying them. I have found no place in the world in which I would rather live.

Some years ago, at a writers' conference in Denver, where I was speaking on the then-fashionable topic of "literature and the land," a man stood in the audience and said, accusingly, What is it about you Western writers and nature? Why do you all write about the land so much? Well, I said, the standard advice you're given in writing classes and textbooks is to write about what you know. If you live in the West, nature is the first thing that greets you in the morning when you go to retrieve your newspaper, nature in the form of a scampering lizard or a jumping cactus, or maybe in a mote of sand that lodges in your eye on a windy day, or maybe in the blistering sun that scorches your fingertips when you open your mailbox. Where are you from? I asked, half expecting the almost obligatory reply. When it came—New York—I went on to say, Well, put it this way: the ice in John Cheever's cocktail glass is the same ice as that choking the Blue River of a January morning, chemically, physically. But culturally they are two very different things, and I'm happier that my ice is tinged with willow bark and perhaps the barest soupçon of beaver urine, and not the gray sludge of the mid-Atlantic seaboard, as inarguably wonderful a city as New York is.

Put another way, once the desert works its way into your soul, you cannot get it out. Once you come to expect blue mountains on your horizon, you cannot be happy in the flatlands or in canyons without hawks.

Having said all that, I need to confess now that I am not a literary desert rat in the manner of an Edward Abbey or Charles Bowden, driven by mad-dog waterless adventure that earns as a by-product a bust in the hall of fame of drylands machismo, a great wing in the library of outback scribbling. Instead, I am your typical conflicted Taoist-aspirant aesthete with passions for punk rock and classical Greek poetry who also happens to like desert places more than any other, who finds solace and succor in the arid venues of the world.

Desert places, I might add, where blue mountains are always within view.

The pieces that follow reflect this liking. I hope that collectively they stand as something of a manifesto: for open land, for suspicious-tasting ice, for the freedom of the highlands and the infernal blaze of the desert in summer. I am no naturalist, either; nor do I really aspire to be one. I am instead a writer interested in nature and in what academics call "cultural geography"; I am less interested in nature and wilderness as abstract good things than in finding ways in which our abstraction-happy culture might make room for the real goods—for wildernesses whose inhabitants can kill and eat us, for unmanaged places in which time has a stop.

In a world gone megalopolitan and biotechnological, such a call may seem, well, quaint. But even quaintness has its uses, and no clock is to be trusted if it cannot be turned back at will.

"Fire in the Sky" first appeared, in different form, in the *Tucson Weekly*. "Desert Winds" first appeared in *Orion* magazine and was reprinted in the 1996 edition of John Murray's annual *American Nature*

Writing, published by Sierra Club Books. "How Baldy Tried to Kill Me" was written for *Mungo Park.* "Blue Mountains Far Away," the introduction to my anthology *The Mountain World* (Sierra Club Books, 2000), first came into being as an essay for *Portland* magazine, although it appears here in much different form; I am grateful to the magazine's editor, Brian Doyle, for having suggested that I write it, as well as for his illuminating essays on William Blake and the pleasures of thought. "Oasis" was written for the Environment Show, a nationally syndicated radio program. "American Byzantium" is the introduction to a collection of images of Las Vegas, as yet unpublished, by the photographer Virgil Hancock. "The Imaginary Atlas" first appeared, in different form, in the *North Dakota Quarterly.* A portion of "The Unknowable Wild" first appeared as the introductory essay to the *Sierra Club Wilderness Calendar 1997.* "Walking" first appeared in *Troika* magazine.

I owe thanks to Robert Hinshaw for friendship and a Swiss retreat, Bryan Oettel and Becky Koh for their encouragement, Bonnie Thompson for her editorial expertise, and Marianne Banes McNamee, my beloved wife, for indulging me in the hair-graying tumult of another book.

Growing Up Nuclear

In the predawn morning of July 16, 1945, a half-mile-long freight train labored up a winding grade between Deming and Las Cruces, New Mexico. As the train topped a tall hill, a flash of light burst high above the eastern horizon, widening and deepening against the blackness of the sky, spreading in all directions, roaring. The light hung in the air for a few seconds, then faded away, leaving on the clouds an eerie imprint.

At first the train's conductor thought that the blazing light was heat lightning. But the winds blew from the wrong direction, and the steadiness of the fire did not match the impetuous here-and-there of a desert electrical storm. He then thought, for a panicked moment, that the light might have been artillery fire aimed at Japanese aircraft, for, rumor had it, the Japanese were about to mount a last-ditch, desperate invasion from nearby Mexico.

In the railyard at Las Cruces the conductor compared his impressions with those of other workers. None of them had a ready explanation for what they had seen. After a few beers and some talk back and forth, they decided it must have been lightning after all, if lightning of a ferocity none of them had seen before.

Standing in his front yard in downtown Tucson half a century later, the conductor, my next-door neighbor for fifteen years, remarks, "It wasn't but a few weeks later that we dropped the A-bombs on the Japs. That's when we figured out that what we saw was some kind of test." He pauses for a moment, remembering. "I can still see it all these years later, that light in the sky."

The Trinity atomic-bomb test, which the conductor had witnessed that morning, was one of many the government had been conducting over the gypsum sands of central New Mexico. Most of those tests were not nearly so visible; most were instead kept as closely guarded secrets. In one, scientists working for the U.S. Army Air Forces attempted to develop a weapon employing hundreds of incendiary charge–laden Mexican free-tailed bats. When released in midair, these bats, the scientists hoped, would take refuge in the rafters and rooftops of Japan's major cities and, when ignited by delayed fuses, would set off a huge firestorm to visit an inferno on the enemy. The experiment was short-lived; the bats instead burned down the laboratory that held them.

But this experiment was of an altogether different magnitude, and it would change history. With it, death left the battlefield and traveled freely everywhere. As former president Herbert Hoover remarked just a few months after the Trinity test, "Despite any sophistries, we have introduced to the world a weapon whose only conceivable purpose is to kill women, children, and civilian men of whole cities." The new weapon unleashed its own firestorm, one whose center was four times the temperature of the sun's at a pressure of 100 billion atmospheres. That storm was visited on Japan, where one eyewitness, a woman named Michiko Ichimaru, reported, "There were dead bodies everywhere. On each street corner we had tubs of water used for putting out fires after the air raids. In one of these small tubs, scarcely large enough for one person, was the body of a desperate man who had sought cool water. There was foam coming from his mouth, but he was not alive."

From the waterless atomic desert of Hiroshima and Nagasaki to the nuclear desert of America is a short step.

Far though it lies from the Fulda Gap and the 38th Parallel, the American West took its place as the chief arena in which the Cold War was waged at home. Today, something like a million Nagasaki-sized explosions—a large portion of the fifty thousand or so nuclear warheads still extant worldwide—lie in atomic embryo throughout the region, squirreled away for another time. That war made of the desert West the Free World's unwilling proving ground, the laboratory for the subterranean thermonuclear explosions and other avatars of what Robert Jay Lifton has called our culture's millennial "immersion in death." Other deserts suffered the same fate. Russia and China tested their thermonuclear arsenals in their drylands, to which hundreds and thousands of leukemia-stricken Central Asians bear witness, while Britain visited its fledgling nuclear might on the deserts of Australia. But nowhere has the Cold War been so manifest as in the American drylands, where it is now being converted from daily reality to nostalgia, enshrined as yet another commodified artifact, turned into a sideshow of living memory in our postmodern circus.

In 1984, an old, blind Hualapai Indian man looked out toward Spirit Mountain, a sacred peak not far from Las Vegas, and spoke, sobbing, of children and grandchildren dead of leukemia and thyroid cancer in the wake of secret nuclear testing the government had conducted for years against enemies half a world away. The old Hualapai's face twisted in pain as he spoke. He had been betrayed, he said. His very faith had been shaken; he was a Mormon, and here in Mormon country, people have a hard time believing that the divinely inspired government of the United States could poison its own people.

But Americans have been poisoned, and burned, and visited with disease because of these tests. Nearly half a million of them had died by the year 2000, the victims of the thousand nuclear explosions set off at the Nevada Test Site in the last half of the twentieth century.

A downwinder, a resident of the Southwest during much of the period when those tests were being conducted, I long ago came to take the atomic issue personally. Born in 1957, the year of Sputnik, I grew up with the Bomb. I was born a dozen years after the dawn of the atomic age, just at the start of the space race, two years after Disneyland opened, three years before Sun City beckoned its first retirees. As a child, I lived on military bases, and I suppose I thought that every normal backyard in America opened onto a view that featured a missile or two, as mine always did. My father served two tours of duty in Vietnam; I marched in antiwar demonstrations at the Pentagon and wrote impassioned antiestablishment screeds in underground newspapers while praying that my turn at the front would not come. My story is by no means unusual; the experiences of millions of Americans intersect with one or another of its main points. I raise it only because I want to emphasize how the Cold War, with its one hundred million dead around the world, defined the culture in which I came of age and matured well into adulthood.

That culture was in turn defined by cartoons and symbols and shorthand, by the pointless exercise of clambering under wooden hinge-top desks for protection from a thermonuclear blast, as if that would help. "Don't get excited or excite others," Bert the

Turtle, the icon of civil defense, instructed us. We did not, as children, disobey him, although nuclear dreams troubled our sleep and nuclear realities brought us endless disappointments. One of them came when I was eleven years old, living in Germany. I waited breathlessly for summer to arrive so that I could attend a Boy Scout jamboree in Bavaria. Our troop made elaborate preparations for the trip, while I raced to complete the requirements for my First Class badge so that I could take part in advanced exercises. At three in the morning on the day we were to leave, my father came into my bedroom. He was dressed in full field gear, a pack on his back, carrying a side arm and rifle. He told me that the jamboree had been canceled, that the two-and-a-half-ton trucks that were to take us into the Alps were needed to transport his unit to the Fulda Gap. The Russians, he added on the way out the door, had just invaded Czechoslovakia.

I have never, I suppose, outgrown my disappointment at missing the jamboree; as I say, I take these things personally. But I coped, and when I went to high school, right outside Washington, D.C., I made a pact with a few friends. When the news of the Bomb's impending arrival finally came over the radio, we decided, we would drop a couple of tabs of LSD, don steel helmets, climb up to the nearest roof, orient ourselves toward the Washington Monument, and wait for the moment when our faces melted, saluting all the while. We agreed with Jim Carroll, the author of the then newly released memoir *The Basketball Di-*

aries, who wrote, "After all these years of worry and nightmares over it . . . I think by now I'd feel very left out if they dropped the bomb and it didn't get me."

The face-melting moment never came, although we practiced the hallucinogenic portion of the drill with regularity. Weaving the Cold War and the Bomb into our odd private mythology, we watched the movies—*Attack of the Fifty Foot Woman, Them!, Night of the Lepus, Tarantula*—and watched the skies, and we waited.

We had long since stopped obeying. We were excited, and we excited others. We grew more excited in 1982, that year of Ground Zero, a time when Ronald Reagan saw fit to joke that American bombers were poised to rain fire on Moscow. I wrote a cycle of death-haunted songs that I am happy to forget now; although technically they were good lyrics, if I do say so, they are by now hopelessly anachronistic, and only a hot revival of the Cold War could make them relevant.

I took it personally, for the Bomb, the culture of the Bomb, deprived me and my agemates for years of a vision of the future. Instead, we had commodity capitalism, production as destruction, an intolerable work world of lies and waste. (And what waste it was. The energy economist Vaclav Smil observes that the development of nuclear weapons has consumed a tenth of the energy used worldwide since 1945.) Ours was a generation looted of its patrimony, as Dwight Eisenhower said in a famous speech of April 16, 1953:

Every gun that is made, every warship launched, every
rocket fired signifies in the final sense a theft from those
who hunger and are not fed, those who are cold and are
not clothed. The world in arms is not spending money
alone. It is spending the sweat of its laborers, the genius
of its scientists, the hopes of its children. This is not a
way of life at all in any true sense. Under the clouds of
war, it is humanity hanging on a cross of iron.

We hung there on that cross for the duration of our
youth, certain that we had no future. We comforted
ourselves with nihilism, with the easiness of seize-
the-day philosophies and other spiritual black holes,
while our elders proved to us that our hopelessness
was well grounded. All we needed for proof was the
folly of Star Wars, another bit of mass-produced
symbolism overlaid on the face of horror. All
we needed was to watch our country, as Edmund
Wilson observed in *The Cold War and the Income
Tax,* lurch about the globe, "self-intoxicated, homi-
cidal and menacing." All we needed were idiotic slo-
gans like "Duck and cover." All we needed was a
nightly session with the nightly news, on which an
army officer, asked to name the most effective
weapons for the next war, replied, "I really can't say.
But I know what weapons they'll be using in the war
after next—bows and arrows."

It is late in 1998 as I write these words. India and
Pakistan are testing nuclear weapons. I sit in an Arizona mountaintop cabin far from the Washington
Monument, no hallucinogens at hand. I am told that
the Cold War is over, has been for years, although no

one ever thought to inform the waiting world that peace had broken out and had been made official.

South Asian leaders, evidently, miss the Cold War. Vladimir Zhirinovsky misses the Cold War. Pat Buchanan misses the Cold War, and so does Gennadi Zyuganov. Ronald Reagan misses missing the Cold War.

To judge by attendance records at the Titan Missile Museum in Green Valley, Arizona, near my Tucson home, plenty of regular folks from around the world feel a little lump in the throat when the atomic era comes to mind. Nearly fifty thousand of them come each year to this decommissioned missile installation, Complex 571-7 on the Pentagon's roster of death-dealing real estate, a stone's throw away from another piece of death-dealing real estate, the bustling retirement community of Green Valley. Deactivated on November 11, 1982, but still owned by the Air Force, the installation is the only place in the United States where the interested traveler can get a close-up look at the weapons that once troubled the sleep of millions of people around the world.

Eighteen such installations—glorified holes in the ground, 146 feet deep, once stuffed full of expensive computer equipment and rocketry—dotted the desert around Tucson during the Cold War's boom years. Built in 1961, this one, called the Copper Penny because of its proximity to a nearby copper mine, is the only one that remains. The others were blown up in 1982, following strategic-arms-limitation talks conducted by Ronald Reagan and a succession of

Soviet leaders after much bellicose prelude. Here four-man crews would sit for twenty-four-hour shifts, awaiting the day when the Reds went a step over the line and all hell would break loose, in the meanwhile baby-sitting a 330,000-pound, 110-foot-long Titan II intercontinental ballistic missile targeted on one of three cities inside the former Soviet Union. Just which ones, no one outside the war room in Washington can say. "The targets," said a museum guide to me, "were known only as 1, 2, and 3. I don't think the boys inside really wanted to know what they were going to vaporize."

Most Americans of a certain age know these steel-case gray and institutional not-quite-lime-green bunkers, but only through films like *War Games*, *Fail-Safe*, *Seven Days in May*, and *Dr. Strangelove*. Fine though they are, those films do not do justice to the retro, paranoia-inducing weirdness of Complex 517-7. The nukeproof burn suits, the glass case full of ignition-switch keys that once promised holocaust, and the red phone, no longer connected, that once rang straight through to Strategic Air Command headquarters are quite enough to make the visitor—again, if he or she is of a certain age—think of taking cover. Even the missile base's motto, *Peregrinamur pro pace*—"We are made to wander for peace"—can make sensitive souls feel uneasy.

As befits an excursion into the Cold War mind-set, the Titan Missile Museum is rich with carefully posted statistics, factoids, time lines. A sign near the museum entrance proudly reports the details of construction: the underground silo and command center used 1,100 tons of rebar, 2,100 cubic yards of concrete, 120 tons of steel beams, 200 tons of electromagnetic lining, and 117 tons of steel rings. The sign announces, with weird pride, the statistics of the Titan II itself, a missile that, after attaining an apogee of 450 miles above the surface of the earth at a cruising speed of 17,000 miles per hour, could strike targets more than 5,000 miles away from its launch site.

Not many of the aptly named Titans were ever built. "We had fifty-four when we started," another guide remarked to me. "We had fifty-four when we were finished. We didn't have to use any of them. After all, we're still here, aren't we?"

The staff of old-timers who entertain questions with bemused and patient smiles are always good for such comforting sentiments, and even a few strange chuckles, as when one warrior replied, when I asked him whether I could photograph the place, "Absolutely, anything you want," all the while shaking his head from side to side in the near-universal gesture meaning no. The guide, a retired Strategic Air Command bomber pilot, then pointed out to me such regalia as the "maximum uncomfortable" rocket-fueling suits installation personnel had to wear when servicing the missile, and the retractable radio antennae designed to rise from a case-hardened underground bunker in the event that a Russian thermonuclear missile landed atop the site and knocked out above-ground communications. "Nuclear near miss?" he crowed. "Failure to respond? Don't look for that in this part of the world."

The high point of the tour came with a hands-on reenactment of the launch sequence that never came, in the case of my tour group commanded by a shy Australian housewife, a tour that comes complete with an eardrum-shattering sequence of bells and klaxons. During this reenactment, the guides shifted disconcertingly from the historical past to the narrative present. On my visit, a guide yelled, "A Soviet ICBM has just obliterated the site above us. We have thirty days of food and water and air left down here. Let's just hope and pray there'll be a world left when we come out."

There was a world left. Stopping for a moment's rest in the shade alongside a radar-equipment trailer, my friend, rock musician and film editor Clif Taylor, grinned and said to no one in particular, "The combination of Cold War fear and modern humor in this place is really weird." A German sugar-beet farmer, born in 1966, rejoined, "In my country, we don't talk about war like this. Maybe things are different if you're the winner."

"This place cost ten million dollars to build back in 1961," our guide, unimpressed by pacifist sentiments, interrupted to say. "It was supposed to be in operation for only ten years. Well, it stayed in service for more than twenty years. I call that a pretty cheap insurance policy."

Asked how much punch the fully armed Titan II packed by way of that insurance, he scratched his head thoughtfully and replied, "Well, the Air Force doesn't want us to discuss payload, but I can get you in the neighborhood of a megaton. A megaton. Compared with this baby, that little thing we dropped on Hiroshima was a firecracker. But that's all over now. People in Moscow can sleep soundly tonight."

Private mythologies are one thing. In the West we have woven the Cold War, uneasily, into our public mythology, and the man is right: people in Moscow, and in New York, and even in Gila Bend can sleep soundly, the night punctuated by the ticking of a Doomsday Clock now set at fourteen minutes to midnight. The cities to which Herbert Hoover adverted remain standing, while the desert countryside of four continents bears the marks of the nuclear era. All appears well, at least on the surface. We can now begin to think about the future. We can now shed our nihilism and go to church.

Or perhaps not. I think of the words of the critic Susan Sontag, who spent her childhood in southern Arizona and who conjured

> a permanent modern scenario: apocalypse looms, and it doesn't occur. . . . Apocalypse has become an event that is happening, and not happening. It may be that some of the most feared events, like those involving the irreparable ruin of the environment, have already happened. But we don't know it yet, because the standards have

changed. Or because we do not have the right indexes for measuring the catastrophe. Or simply because this is a catastrophe in slow motion.

A catastrophe in slow motion: that sounds about right. It has slowed down to a crawl, strangely so. Rockets are aimed at us from Moscow and Alma-Ata and perhaps Urumqi, but they no longer seem real; Pax Coca-Cola reigns over the world; and India and Pakistan are so far away.

But for those of us who grew up in its frightening, long shadow, the Cold War will go on forever, like a desert highway. It endures. It is built into the landscape of the desert, and into our minds: Ground Zero, like the kingdom of heaven, will be forever within us.

Fire in the Sky

Lightning is the lord of everything.
—HERAKLEITOS

I t begins simply, quietly.
A cumulus cloud ambles northeastward from Mexico, bearing water from the Gulf of California and the Sierra Madre. Along its route it collects more water, wringing the already parched desert dry, liberating moisture from swimming pools, center-pivot sprinklers, and irrigation canals. After half a day's march it stumbles into the Mogollon Rim and, too heavy to rise above it, turns southward until it hits the next major barrier, the Santa Catalina Mountains of southern Arizona.

As it fills with water, it grows. Cumulus cloud becomes cumulus congestus, then cumulonimbus, the towering anvil-head formation that marks a midsummer's skyscape in the desert.

Strange things are happening within that mixture of rising air and moisture. At the top of the cloud, thirty thousand feet in the air, the temperature is sixty degrees below zero. There ice crystals, carrying a positive electrical charge, float and collide. At the much warmer bottom, particles of water, also positively charged, swirl about. Somewhere in the middle lies a zone, at about ten degrees Fahrenheit, made up of graupel, ice crystals coated with water and hail that rise and fall with the air currents.

For reasons that atmospheric scientists do not quite understand but are avidly pondering, this graupel has acquired a negative electrical charge somewhere along the way. As it does so, and when, as atmospheric-science researcher Martin Murphy told me with sly vagueness, "other special conditions are met," the action begins. Those "special conditions" include the presence of at least a cubic kilometer of graupel or hail in the cumulonimbus cloud's ten-degree band—enough to cover a city block several miles deep.

Where positively charged ice crystals meet negatively charged graupel, strange magic occurs. First there comes a flicker, a low-powered leader firing downward in an infinitesimally quick burst, perhaps twenty-millionths of a second. It stair-steps downward, forking, streaking several times to the ground at a speed of 460 million feet per second. There a "return stroke"—the flash that we earthbound observers see, and that has yielded the erroneous belief that lightning travels from the ground up—rises to meet it.

The union of upward and downward charges creates an explosion, marked by thunder. That explosion can for an instant create temperatures in excess of fifty thousand degrees Fahrenheit, five times hotter than the surface of the sun. The force of a storm's worth of explosions can equal those of ten Hiroshima-sized atomic bombs.

Thus lightning.

The process is altogether mysterious, and the attempt to decipher its workings has engaged generations of scientists. Today, many atmospheric researchers, engaged in studies of use to military and aviation interests, continue to ponder the basic mechanisms of lightning, even as new discoveries and new mysteries arise. Most recently, tipped off by space-shuttle reconnaissance photographs, many of those researchers are looking into the red and blue flashes called "sprites" that particularly intense storms send high into the atmosphere.

But sprites are symptoms, not causes. The big questions remain as they have for millennia: Where does lightning come from? Why does it exist at all?

The scientists have much material to study. At any given moment, some two thousand thunderstorms are raging across the earth, sending off a hundred flashes of lightning per second, 8.6 million a day, so that the earth from space resembles the paparazzi's gallery at a movie premiere.

Those thunderstorms appear quickly. A cumulus cloud can mushroom into howling fury in only ten minutes. And just when that might occur is anyone's guess. As Chuck Weidman, a University of Arizona professor of atmospheric sciences, says, "Trying to predict when the first lightning bolt will hit is something we just cannot do. We can say there's a cloud out there that meets all requirements to make lightning, but whether it will produce a storm, and when, we don't know."

Weidman is one of several lightning researchers on the faculty of the University of Arizona, where lightning studies have been conducted for half a century; it was here that the noted scientist Leon Salanave did much of the work for his book *Lightning and Its Spectrum*, a standard reference in any storm chaser's library. The university's eminence in lightning studies is in some measure serendipitous. Although Tucson is crawling with people whose living depends in some measure on the mysterious workings of lightning, it is not an especially productive place to study the phenomenon.

"Tucson people like to say that Tucson is the lightning capital of the world," says Weidman, "but it's not really true. If you look at a weather map, you'll see that we're really on the edge of a large unproductive belt"—namely California—"where there's not much lightning most of the year. We don't get all that much ourselves."

Local promoters need not worry about damage to the city's reputation as a storm-watching mecca, however. What draws storm chasers to Tucson, Weidman points out, is that "it's so dry for most of the year that the lightning channel in a cloud is more visible. The clouds are so high that there's plenty of room to see lightning move between the clouds and the ground. That's why the lightning photographs from out here are so spectacular. Plus, lightning photographers are good at getting saguaros and mountains in their shots, making Tucson look more interesting than the more productive places, which are usually farmlands and swamps."

If you want to see a king-hell lightning storm, Weidman counsels, go to Disney World, not Tucson. In central Florida, one recent "mesoscale system"—a massive complex of thunderstorms—produced lightning at the astonishing rate of seven hundred flashes an hour, setting a continental record. Weidman, the author of several scientific papers on lightning, travels there every summer to study the spectrum of lightning at a high-tech research facility on a National Guard base far from any town. From that isolated area, Weidman and his colleagues are able to fire rockets into thunderclouds to trigger lightning, so that it comes crashing down right on top of their monitoring equipment.

"We could do the same thing here, I suppose," he says, "but if we did it on campus we'd bring it down on top of something or someone and do some damage."

Surrounded by computer gear that monitors lightning strikes as they occur across the country, Weidman adds, "Yes, there's more lightning to work with in Florida. But I'm usually too busy watching the equipment to see the really spectacular stuff, like when lightning struck a palm tree right here on campus and set it on fire a couple of years ago."

As a lightning producer, the sky over Arizona ranks far behind Florida, behind Georgia and Alabama, Kansas and Oklahoma, Colorado and Wyoming.

But for all that, lightning is still an important factor in the regional environment, especially because the vast majority of the state's forest fires—and some ten thousand forest fires burn each year in the mountain West—are started by lightning.

Old-time ranchers in particular dreaded the onset of the monsoon season, when lightning fills the Arizona sky, for its advent brought with it the season of destructive cattle stampedes. A reporter for the *Safford Arizonian*, covering an 1899 roundup in the Sulphur Springs Valley, wrote of one such lightning-induced flight:

> I dozed off. . . . I was still semi-conscious when I heard a roar like a mighty tornado, and jumped up as some one said: "Boys, they are gone!" In less than a minute every man is in his saddle and riding . . . after the fleeing herd. The lightning play is grand; electricity everywhere. Flames dance along the horses' manes; balls of fire gleam on ear tip, and by its flashes the boys locate the band before them. . . . Far away in front, above the roar of cattle and thunder, the boys can be heard singing to the maddening herd. As we dash on, the sounds appear to be coming more from the left. They are being pressed around, and soon we see, right in front of the crazed

animals, looking like a ghost, in a long white slicker, his old night horse lunging and fighting for his head, rides Henry Gray, singing, hollowing and swearing by turns. By a concerted action the herd is thrown together and the milling begins. Around and around they go, no beginning, no ending. Just a solid mass, storming and moaning as only stampeded cattle can. Orders are passed around to give more room. The riders fall back and the milling ceases. Now it begins to rain. At the first drop the herd turns and begins drifting the storm, the boys all getting in front endeavoring to hold them back. "Boys, if we can hold them until they all get wet, we will have their company until morning," said our straw boss, Nels Wilson. But alas! It was not to be. Something gives them a scare, and here we go. No sooner are the leaders checked than others turn leader and the whole herd goes thundering after them. And thus the night passes away. The rain is over, but the clouds still hang heavy. An owl in a pine tree makes the night more weird by its howls.

Not content to let the facts speak for themselves, area storytellers added tall elements to what were already powerful realities. Thanks to gifted Pinal County boosters, the area between Florence and Casa Grande especially inspired stories about the powers of local lightning, which, they maintained, magnetized saguaro cacti in weird ways. "All the magnetic cactus in this neighborhood are either positive or negative. One attracts; the other repels," wrote a reporter, tongue in cheek, for the *Florence Tribune,* also in 1899. He continued:

Two tramps passing along the road just above Donneley's a few nights ago took refuge under a bunch of this cactus. One of the men was at once drawn up to and impaled on the sharp blades of the cactus, while its octopus-like arms folded around him crushing him through and into the cactus, where his blood, flesh and bones turned into a pulp very much like ordinary mucilage, which trickled out slowly from the aperture made by the passing in of the man's body. The cactus loses its magnetic power while it is digesting its victim. So we were able to look at this wonderful yet gruesome sight and report these particulars. . . . The body of the other tramp was repelled by the negative cactus and thrown about one hundred feet distant against a positive magnetic cactus where it underwent a similar process to the one just described. We left the sickening scene with sad hearts and with nothing to identify the victims. After and just before a great storm the attractive or repellent power of the cactus is indescribable. Calves, birds and young colts are attracted, impaled, drawn in and quickly converted by the digestive juices of the cactus into the thick mucilaginous substance just described.

The best lightning story I've heard, courtesy of Arizona folklorist Big Jim Griffith, is this: It seems that the uncle of a friend of his, a cowboy in Chihuahua, was out riding fences one day when lightning blew a leg off his horse. The horse keeled over, of course. So the vaquero held up a slab of white cheese and waited for the next stroke of lightning, which immediately followed. The lightning melted the cheese, which he applied to the horse's leg, gluing it back onto the unfortunate steed's body, and off the two rode to shelter.

"The point of the story," Griffith says, "is not really about lightning. It's about the meltability, elasticity, and all-around wonderfulness of Chihuahua cheese."

Lightning is a killer: the National Weather Service reports that nearly 90 people die each year in the United States from direct or indirect strikes. Other federal sources give more generous estimates; the Federal Emergency Management Agency, for instance, reports 150 to 200 deaths annually, with another 750 victims incurring severe injuries. The discrepancies, a recently published insurance-industry study maintains, can be attributed to the fact that lightning death and injury statistics may have been underreported by as much as 50 percent in the last two decades, although why this should be the case is not clear. In any event, another report, this one from Colorado, the state hardest hit by lightning in the West, suggests that lightning-caused injuries requiring hospitalization were underreported by 42 percent from 1982 to 1989, a particularly active storm period.

By any actuarial measure, lightning is the most dangerous force in nature. (A spike in deaths resulting from posthurricane flooding skewed the record in the mid-1990s, but insurance-industry statisticians say that the figures should soon return to normal, giving lightning its numerical supremacy once again.)

Wherever you live in the United States, you are twice as likely to die from lightning as from a tornado, hurricane, or flood. But the bottom-line reality is this: your chances are higher of dying by almost any other means—by a stray bullet, an undercooked cheeseburger, or an errant pickup truck—than of dying by lightning.

Still, lightning should scare you, especially if you are a young man with a blue-collar job or a passion for golf. The vast majority of lightning victims are men under the age of thirty-five who have been either working or playing outside between the hours of noon and six in the evening. Thirty percent of those victims die. Three-fourths of the survivors suffer long-term injuries, including memory loss, sleep disturbance, chronic numbness, muscle spasms, and depression. And many of those survivors die early from burns, cardiac weakness, or systemic failure, especially of the kidneys.

There are some things you can do to keep out of lightning's path. The first thing is to trust your senses. If you can hear thunder, then you are at risk of being hit by lightning, so keep your ears open. Remarks Chuck Weidman, "Lightning is almost always closer than you think it is." And, Martin Murphy rejoins, "Lightning will develop from two to five minutes from the time charging is detected within a cloud. It comes up all of a sudden." When storm clouds move in, head in the opposite direction, for once you are within a dozen miles of a thunderstorm, you stand a chance of being hit by lightning from the overhanging anvil cloud.

Another tactic is to recognize, however grudgingly, that some of the stories your mother told you about lightning are true. Of the number of people whom lightning has zapped in the last decades, two or three annually are people who were holding the phone, engaged in pleasant conversation while the bolts rained down around them. Another two or three were people who were showering or doing the dishes. Still another couple were people who were changing channels or adjusting the fine-tuning on the TV—the most dangerous instrument to be around during a thunderstorm. Stay off the phone and away from water, and turn off the tube.

When a thunderstorm appears, stay well inside, preferably deep within a large building equipped with lightning rods. (Nationally, nearly two-thirds of lightning deaths occur in open fields, under trees, or on open water.) The operative notion is *well inside*: a thirty-year-old Arizona man, reported a 1994 issue of the *Western Journal of Medicine,* was standing near a glass patio door, watching a passing storm, when he felt something he reported to be like "crawling ants" on his face. He had been indirectly hit by lightning, but, unaware of the fact, he went off to bed. The next morning he found that he could not close his right eye or control certain other bodily functions, the aftermath of a neurogenic lesion that, fortunately for him, eventually healed.

If you must stay outdoors during a thunderstorm, seek the lowest ground around—a ditch is ideal—as far away from tall structures and water as you can find. Once there, crouch—do not lie down or touch your head to the ground—in the manner of a baseball catcher, with your hands on your knees. The idea is to have as little of your body in contact with the ground as possible.

Keep away from heavy mechanical equipment, which, the statistics suggest, acts as a magnet for electricity. If you are with a group of people, fan out; lightning probably does not seek out groups deliberately, but it certainly finds them. Wait for a while before venturing outdoors after a storm has passed, to avoid residual lightning.

If you can avoid it, stay out of the sky during thunderstorms. Lightning takes out several small aircraft a year. Bigger aircraft are far safer, even though the National Lightning Detection Board estimates that commercial planes are hit by lightning once apiece each year. Those planes are engineered to withstand the shock of lightning, but every now and then lightning fells one anyway. The largest single lightning-caused crash was on August 2, 1985, when a Delta Lockheed L-1011 jet crashed while landing at Dallas–Fort Worth. In that crash, 135 people died.

And bear in mind that the saw that "lightning never strikes twice in the same place" is flat-out wrong. Lightning often strikes several times in the same area in the course of its being discharged, and these secondary strikes yield more deaths than the primary ones.

If you take no other precautionary measure during a thunderstorm, stay off the links. A huge percentage of lightning strikes occur on golf courses, and the medical literature is full of reports of golfers, caddies, and cart-jockeys being sizzled out on the fairways. It may be that God has a distaste for golfers or that lightning finds a perfect home in those tree-lined, watery expanses, but the odds are against those who insist on playing through in an electrical storm.

Tucson may not lead the nation in lightning production, but the city is a major center for both lightning detection and golf. Leon Byerley, a consultant with Lightning Protection Technology, whose early-warning system for golf courses was featured on the PBS special *Savage Skies*, has much to say about the habits of both lightning and linksters.

"Under the best of circumstances," Byerley remarks, "people won't use their own eyes and ears to know when it's time to come in from a thunderstorm. Golf courses in particular are plagued by this kind of behavior, and that makes sense. If you have golfers putting down $150 to play a game, they'll keep on playing regardless of the weather, and the result is that golf courses all over the country are flooded by lawsuits from bereaved people whose loved ones have been killed by lightning out on the course. Those courses are limiting their liabilities by fulfilling their duty to warn. That's where I come in."

For about $12,000, Byerley's company provides a sensor that can detect lightning within a thirty-mile radius, coupled with a siren system that most of his customers program to sound when lightning has approached within five miles of the course. Even then, Byerley notes, that five-mile warning doesn't give golfers much time to seek shelter. Some golf courses are putting lightning-protection devices on open shelters away from the main clubhouse, but, as signs on Tucson courses warn, these offer inadequate sanctuary from storms.

Byerley counsels that golfers keep an eye on the sky and get off the course as soon as storm clouds appear nearby. "The thinking is, if we have these kinds of warning systems, we may be able to prevent death or injury. But we can't really make all that much of a difference if the golfers choose not to pay attention to them. One golf course in New Mexico that I've worked with, way up in the mountains where there are always thunderstorms hanging around in the summer, reports that half of the golfers ignore the siren when it blows. Here in Tucson, plenty of golfers keep on playing, too. Without common sense, no early-warning system I can build is going to help much.

"I guess you have to conclude," he says, "that human nature is always going to override technology."

I have been dangerously near lightning only a couple of times in my life: once, as a child, in Kansas, when a lightning bolt killed four fellow Boy Scouts camped a few hundred feet from my bivouac, and once on Mount Baldy, Arizona, where a proverbial bolt from the blue shattered a ponderosa pine a couple of hundred feet from where I was standing, coating me with a shower of tiny, sizzling toothpicks.

Those were both exceedingly rare events, neither of them cause for boasting, or even of mention except as curiosities. Yet for all the fear that lightning induces, few people indeed have seen it up close. Fewer still have felt its wrath—and, strangely, none of the professional lightning researchers with whom I spoke had ever themselves met a victim either. Says Chuck Weidman, "I've heard survivors' tales, but not at first hand. A lot of people who claim to have been hit by lightning probably weren't. They were probably near lightning when it struck the ground and got a shock, but that's probably about it. Of course, plenty of people have been hit by lightning directly, but they aren't around to talk about it.

Some years ago the writer Gretel Ehrlich published *A Match to the Heart*, a book reporting her life after she was struck by lightning on the High Plains of Montana. In it, she recalls lying on the ground after the strike, gasping for breath and thinking of "the Buddhist instruction for dying—which position to lie in, which direction to face. Did the 'lion's position' taken by Buddha mean lying on the left or the right?"

We will have to take Ehrlich on faith that this unusually clear thinking really occurred at the time of impact. In the meanwhile, if you hear tell at first hand of someone being struck, write their story down. You will add immeasurably to a scattered and tiny literature.

"We still don't know enough about lightning," Chuck Weidman says, watching the computer screen in his laboratory as icons of bolts dance along a real-time map of southern Arizona. "There are no hard and fast answers to anything about it. There may never be."

For his part, Weidman hopes for a productive season of storms. Nothing would make him happier. "Out here," he says, "you find that people either love lightning or they hate it. I enjoy it, really, just because of the spectacle. I really love watching a good lightning storm.

"But whether you love it or hate it," he says with a knowing grin, "you have to treat it with respect."

Desert Winds

Not long ago a desert-born dust storm rushed by my window, obscuring the view of the Santa Catalina Mountains fifteen miles to the north, of even the alligator junipers in my next-door neighbor's yard. Tawny grains of sand formed dunes in downtown streets, the date palm tree in my yard bent nearly sideways, and a fury of static energy crackled in the air. The sight was impressive. It was even a little frightening, because the season of the great dust storms—from late April until late September—had not yet come. This early ferocity foretokened a hard summer to come, one that only an insurance broker could love.

Deserts are noted, of course, for their lack of water. Deserts are thus thought to lack life—our word comes from the Latin *desertus*, "abandoned," as in Robinson Crusoe's island home—although most of them are really far from desolate. They swarm with life, if the sort of life that snarls, hisses, howls, scratches, and claws. For all that, absences define our deserts, and absences are what we conjure when we mention the word: the writer David Quammen frames the question well by suggesting that "a desert is one of those entities, like virginity and sans serif typefaces, of which the definition must begin with negatives."

But the deserts of the world share one great abundance: wind, and lots of it. What makes them deserts in the first place is not so much the lack of water as the fact that ever-thirsty winds pull such scant rain as falls from the clouds back skyward before it can reach the ground; thus the virga rain phenomenon, where ghostly trails of falling water evaporate thousands of feet above the earth in the thermal-ridden air, as they have been doing this very morning, teasing the mountains with moisture withheld. In windy Bagdad, California, not a drop of rain fell on the earth for 767 days, from September 3, 1912, to October 8, 1914; yet the sky was full of clouds in their season, water kept from the earth by the constant flow of dessicating wind. A similar arid river blows across West Texas, so strong, local legend has it, that if it ever stopped all the cows would fall down.

Dust storms are a common enough occurrence in southern Arizona, especially now that a development boom has scraped off vast swaths of groundcover. They are common enough in every desert of the world. This one's sudden appearance startled me, though, blowing up as it did in a mild season, a time of clement, even sublime weather; its arrival brought to mind the mythographer James G. Frazer's remark in *The Golden Bough*, "Of all natural phenomena, there are, perhaps, none which civilized man feels himself more powerless to influence than the wind." Of the 5,600,000,000,000,000 or so tons of air in the atmosphere, some large part is always whistling down, it seems, on us desert rats, for it is the uneven distribution of solar energy that drives the winds—and solar energy is distributed in an embarrassment of riches across the face of the drylands.

For half the year, the deserts are graced by caressing, soft winds that are nothing less than rejuvenating. In those breezes lie the promise of new life, reverberating through scents like that of the orange blossom—the orange, that heat-loving berry, having been introduced to Europeans in the first century by Greek and Roman travelers to the Thar Desert of India, and reintroduced by Moors into the rich gardens of arid Andalusia, whence most of the Spanish explorers of desert New Spain came. On such days the air hangs in the sky like a loose silk gown, so brilliantly clear, so deep blue, that it seems almost as if you could make out each individual molecule.

But were some master of the Chinese necromantic art of *feng shui*, the alignment of buildings to their environment, to design a house for a Sonoran Desert dweller in the normally clement month of February, the plans would have to be scrapped in two months' time. Come late April, when the orange blossoms fade into memory, ever-intensifying winds announce the advent of summer and, not far behind it, the monsoon season—for, as the Akimel O'odham, the "watercourse people" of the Sonoran Desert, say, "The rain is blind and must be led by the wind."

If you look into the literature of deserts, as I have been doing lately, you will find wind as a constant no less than heat and aridity, and that is just as it should be. One of my favorite passages comes from the naturalist W. H. Hudson's 1917 memoir *Idle Days in Patagonia*, describing the *pampero* that tears across southern Argentina:

> The wind beats incessantly on the exposed roof with a succession of blasts of waves which vary in length and violence, causing all loose parts to vibrate into sound. And the winds are hissing, whimpering, whistling, muttering and murmuring, whining, wailing, howling, shrieking— all the inarticulate sounds uttered by man and beast in states of intense excitement, grief, terror, rage, and what not. And as they sink and swell and are prolonged or shattered into compulsive sobs and moans, and overlap and interweave, acute and shrill and piercing, and deep and low, all together forming a sort of harmony, it seems to express the whole ancient dreadful tragedy of man on earth.

A similar wind, the simoun (the name comes from the Arabic word for poison) shrieks over the Sahara, whipping up sand and dust into fearful, sharp-grained chevaux-de-frise. Herodotus, the great Greek traveler and historian, doubtless got it right when he reported the story of a Libyan army that marched off two and a half millennia ago into the deep Sahara to find and subdue the lord of these storms. The expedition never returned, "disappearing, in battle array, with drums and cymbals beating, into a red cloud of swirling sand." The Assyrians, it is said, did the same, sending squads of archers to combat the approaching clouds. And for good reason: a dust storm buried the city of Ur of the Chaldees for all time, cause enough for a bellicose attitude toward the wind.

Closer to my home, the Tohono O'odham, "people of the stony barren," tell of water serpents that dwell in the boiling summer clouds, bringing rain to the dry earth not in nourishing drops but in great black undulating curtains of water, leaving floods and destruction in their wake. It is no sin to kill such serpents, the O'odham explain, but even their best shamans and archers rarely succeed in doing so.

Ignaz Pfefferkorn spent many years of his life trying to purge that shamanism, that ancient way of knowing nature, as a Jesuit priest among the peoples of the northern Sonoran Desert. He, too, was awed by the power of these great storms:

> Sonora, through these daily rains, receives a pleasant relief from the heat, and at the same time its products are increased. Hence, these rains would surely be considered as priceless blessings of nature were they not always accompanied by the most horrible thunder-storms, which not infrequently do great damage to men and animals in the villages and in the fields. One cannot listen to the continuous crashing of the thunder without shuddering.

At times such thunder-storms bring with them a damag-
ing hail, which destroys all growing things in the field
and garden; or there may occur a ruinous cloudburst, in
Sonora called *culebra de agua,* or water snake, which will
flood over country and villages, devastating them. Sometimes the thunder-storms are accompanied by violent
windstorms and whirlwinds, which lift the sand in a very
thick, twisted column almost to the clouds. Nothing
these whirlwinds seize can withstand their power.

During one such thunderstorm in Arizona in the
summer of 1941, a saltwater clam fell from out of
the sky on a young boy, who was knocked out cold
by the blow. (He fared better than the playwright
Aeschylus, on whose bald head an eagle dropped a
tortoise, killing him instantly.) Scarcely a summer
storm goes by when a pelican or albatross is not
blown from the Pacific or the Gulf of California and
dropped down into the heart of the faraway inland
desert, there indignantly to await what has become
local tradition: a plane ride back to the coast.

It seems that nothing, indeed, can withstand the
power of those great storms. Out of them, after all,
have come gods to terrify humans into obedience; in
the wind-lashed Sinai desert Jehovah first appeared
before Moses as chain lightning, something like the
storm in Ezekiel "coming out of the north, a vast
cloud with flashes of fire and a brilliant light about
it; and within was a radiance of brass, glowing in the
heart of the flames." Such storms are unique among
inorganic phenomena, for they resist the tendency

of all things to slip away into inertia and entropy. Instead, they swell, burst, spawn new storms, and eventually wander off elsewhere to cause new trouble. The last one to visit my home behaved less than divinely: it split a chinaberry tree neatly down the middle, tore up a good section of prickly-pear fence, and sent a well-rooted agave spinning off into the street, all within a minute's time.

Desert tempests have brought down whole governments. They destroyed Ur of the Chaldees; they destroyed Jimmy Carter, who never quite recovered from the hostage-rescue debacle of 1979, when nineteen elite Delta Force soldiers maneuvered their helicopters into a funnel of whirling dust over the barren salt pans of Iran and there met their end. These "dust devils"—the term comes to us by some unknown source from the Indian subcontinent—are an astonishment of nature. If you drive from, say, Phoenix to Los Angeles across the sandy lowlands of the Sonoran and Mojave deserts, you'll count dozens of them on most hot, cloudless days of the year, miniature cyclones dancing to their own music alongside the interstate. When I was six years old, I walked into one as it carved its sinuous course in the gypsum deposits of White Sands, New Mexico, thinking that it would take me off to Oz, a place I had just been reading about. I did not recapitulate Dorothy and Toto's adventures, but I can now take seriously the Southwestern legend that whole flocks of barnyard hens have been swept heavenward through a passing dust devil's fancy. No one has personally seen this occur, of course, but then no one has seen another phenomenon that passes for fact out this way: it's so hot in southern Arizona that chickens lay hard-boiled eggs.

The tallest dust devil ever recorded was spotted in Utah some thirty years ago. It stood about two thousand feet tall, lasted for seven hours—an unusually long life span for what is in essence a tornado—and traveled across the alkali desert for more than forty miles. That it came from the comparatively mild desert of Deseret is no surprise, really, for the Great Basin is the source of most of our continental storm systems. Even the fiercest Saharan sandstorm might be preferable to a day's contending with the basin's fierce winds, which sweep down onto the desert floor from the tall Sierra Nevada and Wasatch mountain fronts, generating howling low-pressure systems like the Washoe. Mark Twain wrote of them, "seriously," that they are "by no means a trifling matter." Not so seriously, he described what a Washoe storm hid within its dust clouds:

> Hats, chickens and parasols sailing in the remote heavens; blankets, tin signs, sagebrush, and shingles a shade lower; doormats and buffalo robes lower still; shovels and coal scuttles on the next grade; glass doors, cats and little children on the next; disrupted lumber yards, light buggies and wheelbarrows on the next; and down only thirty or forty feet above ground was a scurrying storm of emigrating roofs and vacant lots.

On the fringe of the Great Basin lies the resort town of Palm Springs, California, where I happened to spend a summer night not long ago. Trying to reach my room from the lobby, I was buffeted from one end of a Motel 6 parking lot to another by midnight winds that screamed down through the San Gorgonio Pass—the site, appropriately enough, of a giant windmill field, one of the West's countless monuments to surrealism. As I careened off Dumpsters and fire hydrants, I wondered why on earth wealthy celebrities like Jerry Lewis, Steve Allen, Gerald Ford, and Bob Hope should wish to spend their waning days surrounded by such gales. Perhaps, I concluded, those winds sharpen the edge somehow, rather like those sandblasted Egyptian pyramids are thought to do in certain mystical circles.

Cousins to the *maloja* of the Swiss Alps, the *yama oroshi* of Japan, and the *reshabar* of the southern Caucasus, the winds that played parking-lot pinball with me are known to Americans as the Santa Anas. The mechanism that drives them works like this: on warm days the air rises uphill from valley floors, and then cools as it ascends, creating an upward-downward (anabatic-katabatic) wind flow. In the case of the Santa Anas, high pressure over Utah and Nevada causes air to spill off the Mojave Desert, rushing over the Pacific coastal range and onto the coastal lowlands. The coastal air is robbed of humidity by this thirsty invader and fills with static electricity. As they envelop desert and littoral alike, the Santa Anas create an atmosphere of impending doom. During their season, as Raymond Chandler wrote in his famous story "Red Wind," "Meek little wives feel the edge of the carving knife and study their husbands' necks. Anything can happen."

Anything can, and it usually does. Most heart attacks and strokes among desert dwellers occur when the wind is blowing at near force 4 or 5 on the Beaufort scale, or eleven to twenty-one miles per hour, about the average for a Santa Ana day. And statistics compiled by the Los Angeles Police Department demonstrate that homicide rates, already fantastically high in southern California, double when the desert winds are blowing. (In the Gobi the winds rush along at between fifteen and twenty-five miles an hour for weeks at a time. I wonder why contemporary Mongolians do not massacre each other daily, but I understand better why the bloodthirsty Golden Horde exploded from out of the high steppes a millennium ago.) In Pfefferkorn's time, Spanish defendants could cite the wind as an extenuating circumstance in homicide trials. The dust devil, it would seem, made them do it.

Poison gusts, homicide, despair. The desert winds grind down mountains, scrub boulders down to pavement and dust, lay bare the bleak flats of the Bisti badlands of the Navajo nation, the clean-scoured salt pans of the Takla Makan. Why ever would anyone choose to live among these all-devouring currents?

Perhaps because, eternal optimists, we desert rats remember the gentle days, the scent of birthing orange buds and new bunchgrass, days when the calls of birds and coyotes linger in the soft, still air. Even after escaping what turned out to be the hottest summer in recorded Sonoran Desert climatic history for a few weeks in August 1994, I found myself missing the *culebras de agua* and howling winds when I should have been thanking my stars for a sojourn in the temperate Ish River country. Call it perverse, but I was glad to descend again into the familiar furnace of the Great American Desert, even glad to see one of its westernmost gateways down the decidedly un-friendly—for so Buck Owens instructs us—streets of Bakersfield, alongside which dust devils danced.

The desert winds do not tolerate our inexperience, and they assure us of our many imperfections. They test us and find us wanting. But they keep those of us who live among them guessing, never quite certain of what the next subtle shift of current will bring: a scent from paradise, or a blast from the inferno.

Finding the Garden

Early September, midafternoon. The temperature on the desert floor seven thousand feet below hovers near the century mark, but the rocky ledge on which I sit is a comfortable twenty-five degrees cooler. Skirls and banners of storm clouds drift through the canyons that wind up to this spot, favoring the ground with an occasional splash of rain, fast and furious. Their advance is punctuated by blasts of cool air that fulfill the Akimel O'odham adage "The rain is blind and must be led by the wind."

I often come to this spit of granite high in the Santa Catalina Mountains north of Tucson, the desert city in which I make my home. For three decades I have wandered their cactus-studded forerange of crumbling, banded gray gneiss, scrambled through channels that falling water has carved over the millennia, picked my way over talus slopes and volcanic scree a hundred million years old, finally to arrive at this magical place. Not that every experience must be so trying a test of physical fitness: a narrow two-lane highway, built by convict labor in the 1930s, passes within a hundred feet.

My sanctuary is a maze of weathered sandstone and granite, a battlement of what geologists call hoodoos, rock columns shaped by the fanciful sculpting of the winds. The largest of these hoodoos, Duck Rock, to my immediate left, towers a hundred feet over the lip of thousand-foot-deep Molino Canyon. (When I first saw Duck Rock, it was festooned with a trio of climbers who seemed unconcerned that a quarter mile of air separated them from the nearest horizontal ground.) Other hoodoos bear similar names: Nixon Head, as I dubbed it for its marked resemblance to the former president in profile; the Three Sisters, a triple-pronged outcrop of red sandstone; the Apache, its sharp angles suggesting the Roman noses and high cheekbones of that famous people.

These hoodoos are rare enough in nature, found here and there in deserts throughout the world. These mountains are rare enough, too: an urban wilderness in the very backyard of one of the nation's fastest-growing cities, a quarter of a million acres of primal land bisected by only a thin ribbon of road that, on this rainy day, only a handful of automobiles have negotiated. This is a place to come to be alone, far removed from the pressures of city life. Barring the occasional sputter of a car engine or the whine of a jet plane high overhead, this is how the world might have been a hundred thousand years ago.

These mountains are my garden.

Garden: the open world, tended by humankind, in the original sense of the ancient Persian term from which our word *paradise* derives. I use the possessive adjective "my" advisedly. I mean not ownership but responsibility. I mean nothing more than obligation, quite unlike an old woman whose memoirs I edited nearly twenty years ago, who insisted on deeming the birds and animals surrounding her desert hideaway "my roadrunners," "my chipmunks," and so forth. (She even went so far as to call the neighboring ranchhands "my Mexicans.") Her book, published by a well-known New York house, went on to become a steady seller, which has never ceased to amaze me. She was a passable bird-watcher, but her attitude kept her from being someone you'd want to go birding with.

The sort of responsibility, of obligation that I mean stands as one of the chief tenets of what ecologists call "bioregionalism." The notion had not been broadly articulated—or at least I had not heard of it—when I first staked my claim to this small corner of the Santa Catalina Mountains, but its program is modest enough: one finds a special place in nature, determines that he or she will protect that place, deeply studies its natural and human history in the field and on the printed page, visits it often, observes it thoroughly, and preserves it from threat.

This place need not be wilderness. A New Yorker might adopt a few square feet of Central Park, a Washingtonian a patch of dogwood along the C&O Canal. A southerner might take on a patch of cypress forest or an Appalachian hillside, a Kansan a piece of bottomland along one of that state's delicate streams, an Oregonian a stretch of rocky beach. What matters is that the place becomes your own, that it, too, becomes your garden.

The gardener who merrily works a patch of soil throughout the year—that stock character in so many English novels of country life—requires good tools: a sturdy hoe and trowel, work gloves, a strong set of knees. The gardener who cultivates a patch of the wild world needs fewer formal tools. A good pair of walking shoes, a notebook, a set of binoculars, and a canteen full of water make up my normal provisions.

Foremost, both kinds of gardeners require a knowledge born of observation and experience. Some of it comes from books. One that every gardener of the wild or tame should have is the eminent English biologist Gerald Durrell's *The Amateur Naturalist,* which is of equal service to desert rat, shore dweller, and woodland walker alike. More specialized titles are available for different climates and life zones; the Audubon, Sierra Club, and Houghton Mifflin guidebooks to the birds, trees, animals, and flowers of different parts of the country can all be highly recommended.

Arid-lands ecologist Peter Warshall has provided gardeners with other tools, in the form of a set of provocative questions. Among them, Warshall asks, "Where does the water you drink come from?" A New Yorker who pursues this question will eventually draw a line to the Catskills, a resident of Los Angeles to the ever-shrinking Colorado River, a citizen of Denver to mountain lakes high in the Rockies. Whatever the answer, the quest to locate it is an education in itself.

A second, equally broad question asks that the gardener name the major plant and animal species that inhabit his or her chosen corner of the world. A resident of the Great Plains might point to tallgrass, sagebrush, antelope, and deer, and can spend a lifetime looking into the relationship each has with the others. From my aerie here in the Upper Sonoran Desert, I can answer this question by pointing out an abundance of interwoven species: mesquite and barrel cacti, tarantulas (two days ago I came across the largest I had ever seen, the size of a softball) and diamondback rattlesnakes, Gambel's quail and Anna's hummingbirds, fellow citizens.

Our objects of study can be as deep or as broad as we like. Following Warshall, we can take the large view by cataloging the acts of God and natural events that most influence life in our gardens: fire, lightning, hurricanes, tornados, fog, drought. Or we can seek out minute details, through such exercises as analyzing the soil series on which we stand. (In my case this is a loose agglomerate of mineral-rich sands atop a cementlike layer of clay called caliche, so hard that the roots of only one species of desert tree can penetrate it. This is the chief reason why houses in this part of the country lack basements.)

The path to knowledge is endless. A good gardener, whether a specialist in a few varieties of roses or in a patch of cloud-swathed mountains, always finds more to learn. The reward is the study itself, for only by our close observation and questioning does nature begin to yield up some of its manifold mysteries.

We study, and we learn. Some of our knowledge can and should be shared, hence the vast library of books about American natural history—the genre of literature, above any other, in which our nation's writers have always excelled.

But some of that knowledge, I think, should be held in reserve, kept in what Jack Kerouac called our "mad, secret notebooks." Without some mystery, after all, our world would be a passionless, tedious place. As he so often did, Henry David Thoreau provides a talisman, in a quotation so often repeated that it has come to be a cliché:

> At the same time that we are earnest to explore and learn all things, we require that all things be mysterious and unexplorable, that land and sea be infinitely wild, unsurveyed and unfathomed by us. . . . We need to witness our own limits transgressed, and some life pasturing freely where we will never wander.

Some of what we learn in our gardens, in other words, belongs in a file marked "Top Secret." By way of example, I have an acquaintance who has chosen a few square miles of the Grand Canyon as his private garden. They lie far from roads and even maintained trails, and for a few weeks of each year he disappears into their depths, returning to civilization with a good tan and leg muscles that resemble oak branches. We occasionally share notes, but our conversations are kept deliberately vague. He has his place, after all, and I have mine.

When we last spoke, my acquaintance mentioned that he had traced a small stream to its source near the eight-thousand-foot-high rim of the canyon. There he found a cavern, and inside it a vast underground lake that appeared on no map. (The Grand Canyon has yet to be completely explored and cataloged, and its students turn up new caves, rock ledges, and springs every year.) The geology of the region is, at least in theory, right for such a lake, but none has ever been found in the hundred or so years that modern scientists have probed the canyon's depths. As far as my acquaintance is concerned, there is no reason to spread the word about the location of this one.

It is selfish, perhaps even arrogant, to withhold such knowledge, some may argue. But I suspect that when the lake's location is eventually revealed, as it is sure to be, it will be turned into a commodity, with the inevitable guided tours, snack bars, and busloads of visitors to make a circus of a once-quiet spot. All that is reason enough to hold one's tongue.

No, it is better to keep a few secrets. One night years ago, I sat in my own garden, admiring the full moon, whose light bathed the mountains. In the corner of my vision came a rustling two hundred or so yards distant. As I looked more closely, I made out the shape first of a mountain lion, and then of two cubs who frisked after her. Like hoodoos and underground lakes, mountain lions are lamentably rare in this part of the world. Many are shot on sight.

But not these. I held my breath and waited for them to cross into the next canyon, a trek that seemed to stretch out for hours but in fact lasted only a minute or two. They paused every now and again to sniff the air, and I am quite certain they smelled a human in that soft wind. But they went on. I have seen them since, I think, the cubs now full grown with cubs of their own, stalking this same well-traveled mound of granite.

Just where they live, in that secret garden, I will never tell.

How Baldy Tried to Kill Me

On a tattered nineteenth-century military map of Arizona's White Mountains, the state's second-highest summit bears a name that, so far as I know, appears on no other chart: "Home of the Winds." This is probably the cartographer's poetic invention, for modern Apaches call the 11,403-foot-tall peak Dzil Ligai, "mountain of white rock," an accurate enough description of the exposed granite summit that Anglos call Mount Baldy, a name less pretty but just as prosaic as the Apache.

It is bald, to be sure. It is also windy, the abode of howling gales. For all that, I've given other names to Mount Baldy over the years, names more suited to a pro wrestler than a stately snow-capped rise: The Berserker. The Unforgiver of Black River. Geronimo's Revenge. Mount Psycho.

They are hard names, I know, but fair ones. Fair because almost every time I have tried to climb it, Mount Baldy has tried to terminate my tenure on this green and lovely earth.

I first came to the mountain in 1975. I found it breathtakingly beautiful, a standout in a state full of picturesque places—but, at first glance, strangely unimpressive. For one thing, it doesn't look like much of a mountain: beautiful though it is, Baldy rises gently above an 8,000-foot plateau, with no eye-popping precipices or fearsome crags to arrest the viewer. For another, it sports a well-maintained trail that winds pleasantly over eight and a half miles through pine forests and alpine meadows gushing with springs. There's no need for ropes or pitons on this scenic and seemingly unscary mountain, scarcely even need to take along a topo map, and hundreds of people of all ages climb Baldy every year without incident.

But only a few of them ever make it to the very top. Just within the borders of the White Mountain Apache Reservation, the summit is closed to non-Apaches; access to it is blocked by a cattle fence. In Apache belief, mountaintops are the dwelling of spirits called *gan*, who protect wild animals and bedevil most other mortals. Few Apaches go to the top of Dzil Ligai, except for religious purposes. Few, at least of my acquaintance, speak openly of the *gan*, who are dangerous and volatile, and who visit disease and madness on anyone who angers them.

The ascent of Baldy is easy, but the *gan* work hard to keep nosy foreigners away, hard enough to change my opinion of the mountain. It definitely impresses me now.

* * *

That first trek up Baldy began pleasantly enough. The trail was easy, the sky deep blue, the air warm. The closer I got to the summit, however, the faster omens came. At a narrow pass where the trees end, at about 10,000 feet, I had to throw myself to the ground to avoid a collision with a golden eagle, nearly earthbound by the weight of a fat jackrabbit it clutched in its talons. An ancient Greek would have erected an impromptu shrine to the gods on the spot and turned tail, but I blithely proceeded. A mile up the trail I met with another visitation from the heavens: a literal bolt from the blue that sent a fifty-foot-tall ponderosa pine flying apart in countless toothpicks. (I plucked one from my hair and still keep it as a souvenir.) The explosion was immediately followed by a phenomenon unique, I believe, to the desert: drenching rain falling without a cloud in sight.

I kept right on going for another half mile, soaked but not broken, as the mountain began to deliver views extending a hundred miles in every direction. Rounding a bend, I came within sniffing distance of an adult black bear—which is to say, I smelled it, and I'm sure it smelled me. Whether male or female I did not ascertain, and I call it an adult only because of what then seemed to me to be its monumental size. We stood there, bear and I, perhaps seventy feet apart (distances are hard to measure in such circumstances), for perhaps five minutes (ditto units of time), until the bear, evidently bored with the proceedings, turned and lumbered off down a nearby draw.

And at that, the cloudless rain pouring off my shoulders, I turned and ran eight miles down Baldy without stopping, thankful that I had had the chance to see lightning up close and a black bear in the wild, thankful that the lightning and the black bear had had the chance to kill me and did not. It was quite enough for one day.

A few years later I returned to Baldy for another try. As before, the day began beautifully. As before, a thousand feet below the summit a fierce rain began to fall. Inasmuch as it was October, a dry season in Arizona, I had not packed rain gear, a datum the *gan* did not overlook. The rain and hail came crashing down so hard on stones in the narrow draw that little bits of mica blew off and filled the air with a brilliant shrapnel—not enough to kill a person, but perhaps enough to put an eye out. It was impossible to proceed under the circumstances, and all too easy to die of exposure.

I took shelter under a chaos of boulders that shielded a cave entrance. The overhang seemed a fine place to wait out the storm, and I sat there eating bread and salami as lightning crashed down until I heard snuffles coming from somewhere within the cave—noises that seemed to grow louder with each passing moment. I weighed my options and called out to unknown beast and *gan* alike, "Hey, damn it, you've got the wrong guy!"

This was craven and abject behavior, I know. But I had a legitimate point: while the Apaches—and Arizona's wildlife, for that matter—were suffering the greatest injustices done to them, my ancestors were in Ireland fighting desperate battles of their own. Whatever evils had happened in Baldy's shadow were not my bloodline's fault.

Still, the snuffling did not stop. Neither did the cold rain, and once again I found myself running down the mountain, this time so quickly and furiously that my battered ankles swelled up for weeks afterward to remind me of my misadventure.

For the next several years I confined myself to Baldy's lower slopes, following the tracery of the Little Colorado River's sources, content to collect rivers instead of summits. Every now and again, in all seasons, I ventured closer to the top, and each time the story was the same: rain, snow, hail, and always those great bolts of lightning.

I had begun, as you might expect, to take the mountain's behavior personally. But I still kept at it, mindful of Neville Shulman's remark, in his book *Zen in the Art of Climbing Mountains,* that "nothing is possible without three essential elements: a great root of faith, a great ball of doubt, and fierce tenacity of purpose." I had little faith that I would ever make it to Baldy's summit—as far, that is, as I was permitted to go. I had much doubt, but also a deep well of tenacity, mulishness that the *gan* rewarded by finally allowing me to ascend Baldy twenty-two years after my first attempt, in March 1997. When I climbed past the stump of that lightning-shattered ponderosa, no eagles or bears or bolts from heaven challenged me. I even came within sight of the gate leading through the fence into the Apache nation and the abode of the *gan*, the home of the winds. A few drops of rain fell, but softly.

Not wanting to push my luck, I left a hawk feather on a rock beside the trail, promised the mountain to speak of it by more kindly names, and turned back, walking along under a clear blue sky.

Blue Mountains Far Away

The din of the dusty world and the locked-in-ness of human habitations are what human nature habitually abhors; while, on the contrary, haze, mist, and the haunting spirits of the mountains are what human nature seeks, and yet can rarely find.

—KUO HSI

Was the earth created with or without mountains? A strange question, perhaps, but one that nonetheless occupied the residents of the Jesuit college of Coimbre, France, for the better part of the year 1592, when the gold-rich mountains of the newfound Americas and of Asia were much on the European mind.

Using twists and turns of logic and complex arguments of faith, the seminarians argued pro and con, invoking such contradictory sources as their near contemporary Saint John of the Cross, who urged seekers after the truth to retreat to "solitary places, which tend to lift up the soul to God, like mountains, which furnish no resources for worldly recreations," and the Old Testament prophets, who conversely regarded mountains as frightful places capable of settlement only by Yahweh and assorted demons. But in the end, having determined that the mountains brought living humans as close as they could ever come to the heavens, the Jesuits of Coimbre ruled that mountains were evidence of the earth's perfection as the creation of an infallible God. So the matter rested. Only a century later would it be revived, briefly, when the Protestant theologian Thomas Burnet countered that the earth was inherently "confused by Nature" and that the mountains were "Ruines and Rubbish on a dirty little planet."

Ruins and rubbish, the flatlander's worldview, the notions of someone who has little use for alternate realities. We have since his time made room in our mental and spiritual worlds for mountains, and Burnet has few modern supporters, I suspect, with the notable exception of the confirmed city dweller and sophisticate Roland Barthes, a sometimes Catholic, sometimes Marxist, always interesting literary critic who sniffed at the "Helvetico-Protestant morality" of mountain lovers while arguing that qualities like verticality, "so contrary to the bliss of travel," are the heaven of the Michelin Blue Guide but the hell of ordinary mortals. Poor misguided soul, Barthes was run down while trying to cross a busy Paris street, miles away from the nearest mountain of any account, safe from the imagined terrors of the Alps.

A strange matter, as I say: swirling, heated, passionate arguments over the value and even validity of some of the planet's most characteristic landmasses. We are fortunate to live in a time when the holiness of mountains is almost a given, as the world's religions have always taken it to be. And for good reason: who, standing on that point of land where Meriwether Lewis exclaimed, "Ocian in view," and taking in the vast magnificent sweep of the central Cascades, could not believe that there, up on 12,307-foot Mount Adams or 14,410-foot Mount Rainier, lies a threshold of heaven? There on those peaks, some native peoples of the Pacific Northwest say, stands the abode of the spirits, of fierce winds, of the very Creator. There, Warm Springs storyteller Lucy Miller told the anthropologist Theodora Kroeber, the gods wrestled as Coyote, the Trickster, mightily conspired to keep Mount Adams and Mount Hood from killing each other in a long-ago time. There the earth shook so badly that the First People all disappeared, leaving only the Klah Klahnee, the Three Sisters, behind to guide the next people to their new homeland.

On another volcanic mountain half a world away—one that probably does not exist in time or space but only in metaphor—Saint Paul rose to behold his God, pointing the way to yet another new homeland. And on still another mountain, a 2,510-

foot cinder cone called Cruachán Aigle, Saint Patrick strode forth to conquer the citadel of the ancient Irish harvest god. He did so, and the mountain, now called Croagh Patrick, is now Ireland's holiest peak. As the anthropologist Lawrence Taylor observes in his study of Irish Catholic pilgrimage *Occasions of Faith*, Patrick played on powerful memories when he conquered that height, sacred before as now, driving away the great bird and the monster serpent who guarded its summit. Mountains, along with wells and caves, were the loci for the Christianization of Ireland, and today thousands of people retrace Patrick's steps on the first Sunday of August.

They are wild places, those mountains, and terrifying. There is something about mountains that sends humans into states of consciousness—fearful, reverential, even awestruck—that are far from our normal modes of being. Some of the reasons are obvious, even deceptively so. As the Jesuits of Coimbre observed, for believers mountains are the closest points on the planet to the abodes of the gods, connecting the spirit world with our own. Mountains hold obvious dominion over the land, stern royalty gazing down on their lowly subjects. And, of course, mountains are high places, and many people fear heights, although a current psychiatric index will show you that many more people fear, in descending order, animals, the sight of blood, and being penned up in enclosed spaces.

From terror grows a kind of grace. It is no surprise, I think, that Saint Francis's notions of "tendance and comforting" should have arisen in the mountains through which he walked, ideas he elaborated while coursing the craggy spine of the Apennines on the way from Assisi to La Verna, for without such kindness, a contemporary remarked, "in those desolate places man could not live." Grace indeed: the nature of mountains embodies the gift by which God enables us to live holy lives, Saint Francis said. They change our being. Thus, as John Muir observed at the beginning of this chewed-up age, "thousands of tired, nerve-shaken, over-civilized people are beginning to find out that going to the mountains is going home."

In mountains were nourished the great religions of the world, nearly all born in the deserts but raised in the high country. The environmental psychologist Bernard S. Aaronson has noted that "the traditional association of mountain tops with the abode of Deity may be less because they are higher than the areas around them than because they make possible those experiences of expanded depth in which the self can invest itself in the world around it and ex- pand across the valleys," a feeling that resembles nothing so much as extrasensory perception. That is just the feeling experienced by human beings deprived of oxygen, a sure step toward coma, and by those who have survived close encounters with death: most mountain climbers, in other words.

Countless alpinists report returning from the mountains filled with an inexplicable sense of inner peace born of that sensory sharpening, filled with something approaching the religious thump on the head that Buddhists call satori, like Maurice Herzog's epiphany atop the 26,334-foot summit of Annapurna: "I had a vision of the life of men. Those who are leaving it for ever are never alone. Resting against the mountain, which was watching over me, I discovered horizons I had never seen. There at my feet, on those vast plains, millions of beings were following a destiny they had not chosen. There is a supernatural power in those close to death." And in those, we might say, who venture close to it, as you will read in the pages of Neville Shulman's memoir *Zen in the Art of Climbing Mountains*, an account of terror and redemption on the north face of 15,771-foot Mont Blanc, and in the ninth-century Japanese account of a Buddhist monk named Shodo who climbed the volcanic peak Nantaizan to confront his mortality:

> "If I do not reach the top of this mountain, I will never be able to attain Awakening!" After having said these words he moved across the glistening snow and walked on young shoots glimmering like jewels. When he had ascended halfway, all strength left him. He rested for two days and then climbed to the peak. His joy there was complete, like that of a dream: his dizziness portended the Awakening.

In the mountains the eyes become clearer, it seems, the ears more finely tuned; the customary flavors of food take on new nuances; the calls of birds compose a richer music. The first European known to have climbed a mountain for the sheer pleasure of it, the Italian poet Petrarch (1304–1374), devoted many pages of his journals to describing the odd sensations that overcame him in the highlands, especially on seeing a glacier-lit rainbow atop the small alp Ventoux: "I stood as one stupefied. I looked down and saw that the clouds lay beneath my feet. I felt as if another."

As if another, indeed. The English Catholic mystic Dom John Chapman calls the sense of mountains "unearthly and expanding," echoing the English traveler Freya Stark's notion that the mountains are moving vortexes of energy on a spinning globe— another strange idea, on the face of it, but one that has considerable attraction when you consider that everything on the planet is indeed constantly in motion. I have experienced that "unearthly and expanding" sense on a number of mountaintops: on the Zugspitze, in the Bavarian Alps; on Mount Evans, one of Colorado's "fourteeners"; on Mount Rainier and, just a few weeks before it blew, on Mount Saint Helens; and, most profoundly, atop Copperas Peak, an otherwise unimposing mountain in southwestern New Mexico that overlooks the rushing headwaters of the Gila River, three streams that pour down from the surrounding highlands and unite two thousand sheer feet below.

The vista there is dizzying. "Don't go into the Gila if you're scared of heights," a waitress in Silver City said to me on my first visit there, after watching me puzzle over a topographic map, trying to make sense out of the jumble of mountains that fold and unfold, accordionlike, across the landscape. (The Japanese Zen master Dōgen Kigen evoked a similarly topsy-turvy geology when he wrote in his *Mountain Sutra*, "As for mountains, there are mountains hidden in jewels; there are mountains hidden in marshes, mountains hidden in the sky; there are mountains hidden in mountains. There is a study of mountains hidden in hiddenness.") The waitress had a point. These streams and their feeders arise in springs and ice caves atop towering ranges—the Mogollon, Black, and Pinos Altos Mountains—that ring the Gila Basin on the immediate west side of the Continental Divide. The vertiginous roads that lead over them and down to the water would, I imagine, be an acrophobiac's worst nightmare. Atop Copperas Peak, perched tentatively on a narrow shelf of granite with its hundred-mile view on all sides, you have the impression that the horizon is limitless, and that you, mere human, are tiny to the point of insignificance.

There is much value in that humbling experience. In their mountain-studded Alaska homeland, the anthropologist Richard Nelson has observed, Koyukon children learn their place in the order of things from geomorphology itself, having been instructed that they are not to argue over the respective merits of mountains or to compare their sizes.

"Your mouth is too small," an offending child will be scolded, meaning that we humans cannot possibly comprehend the vastness of nature. Similarly, the O'od no'ok, or Mountain Pima, of northern Mexico liken themselves to ants who crawl along the ragged canyons and massifs of the western Sierra Madre, singing traditional songs that reinforce the notion of our tininess against the heights. Buddha was likely getting at the same idea when he observed, "In the high places of the earth the being is better to look at himself in the face and learn the truth and true proportion of things."

Terror, vertigo, insignificance: it is odd, perhaps, that these fundamentally dehumanizing elements should lead to the sublime state that characterizes our best spiritual impulses. The human mind is made up of odd stuff, however, and susceptible to seeing in the land whatever it chooses to. In the mountains, those frightening places, it locates the deities. There is no mountain landscape in the world that is not heavily invested with gods, sometimes from many traditions. Chomolungma, or Everest, is sacred to Hindus, Buddhists, Taoists, and Confucianists alike. Similarly, Mount Cuchama, near San Diego, is a mountain island sacred to the now-dispersed Luiseño and Diegueño Indians of the California coast, but also to the far-inland Cocopa, Quechan, and Chemehuevi peoples, for whom the distant mountain, rising above the sere desert floor, was a place of pilgrimage.

Saint Theodoros, a Byzantine mystic, held that "a mountain is the image of the soul rising in meditation." The metaphor is apt. Surely Jesus knew the power of landscape when he took up his position on an unnamed mountainside—perhaps it was Tabor, the site of his transfiguration—to give the Sermon on the Mount. There Jesus commanded a sweeping view of his followers and the valley below them while enjoying a steep, craggy backdrop that symbolically projected him into heaven, ascending to attain the ethereal, the clarity, the shudder that the theologian Rudolf Otto finds in the presence of what he calls the "numinous," lying at the base of all religious impulse. It is no accident, I think, that Jesus chose a mountain site on which to deliver his most powerful address: from on high, there next to God, he spoke of good and evil, of loving one's enemies, of doing's one part in bringing peace to the world. From on high, he taught his followers how to pray.

Just so, throughout time, in religious traditions the world over, holy people have taken themselves into hermitage in the mountains, there to let their souls rise. Just so, throughout time, we have found peace and spiritual succor in the highlands of the world, where, the Hindu Puranas promise, "As the dew is dried up by the morning sun, so are the sins of mankind dried up by the sight of the mountains." Just so, the world over, the architecture of the sacred aims to emulate mountains, as with the ziggurats of Babylon, which bore names like House of the Mountain and Mountain of God; the pyramids of

Egypt, the temples of Jerusalem, the stupas of Tibet, the Gothic cathedrals of Europe; even, in this money-worshiping age, the skyscrapers of our urban centers. It is tempting to think that God demolished the Tower of Babel not out of anger for its builders' having attempted to unite humans with their maker but for their hubris in trying to re-create what nature takes millions of years of geological evolution to accomplish: a mountain piercing the heavens.

We cannot undo two million years of our own primate evolution to dissolve the fears and emotions that lie at the center of our beings. Rollercoasters, tall buildings, and good portions of the films *Cliffhanger* and *The Eiger Sanction* can still produce those beads of sweat that proclaim our fragility, even though we pretend to be masters of our world. And in that pretense, overlooking the tininess of which those Koyukon mothers so wisely speak, we are increasingly placing the world's mountains at risk.

Sometimes we do so out of greed. Where two thousand years ago Greek priests climbed the slopes of Olympus and Parnassus to search for signs of lightning, indications that burnt offerings were propitious and prayers to the gods most likely to be heard, now their descendants build ski lodges. Indian casinos now lie spattered among the once-sacred mountains of Arizona, California, New Mexico.

And sometimes, with less damage to be sure, we do so out of mere vanity, out of the misplaced drive to conquer nature. N. E. Odell, who accompanied the tragic Mallory expedition to Everest in 1924, wondered whether it were right to climb it: "If it was indeed the sacred ground of Chomolungma, Goddess Mother of the Mountain Snows, had we violated it—was I now violating it?" Today, in the race to deprive the planet of all its mysteries, such questions of propriety are laid aside. Not long ago the famed alpinist Reinhold Messner, having secured permission from Chinese authorities glad to offend Tibetan sensibilities, announced his plan to climb Kailas, the holiest of holy mountains to untold millions of people, despite warnings that to do so would be to profane it.

Whether we climb them or view them from afar, they continue to pull at us, calling us home, those mountains. Watching their peaks pierce the sky, here in the Sonoran Desert, I count myself fortunate to have their sanctuary, their daily reminder of the generosity of the land, and to be able to yield again to tininess, even to terror, and to the ever-expanding universe that lies in the ranges beyond.

Four Rivers

In the middle of the Piazza Navona of Rome stands one of the finest monuments to the Renaissance mind ever made: Gian Lorenzo Bernini's Fountain of the Four Rivers.

A monument in a city full of monuments, it does not seek to overwhelm or awe, as do constructions like the towering vault of Saint Peter's or the needling spire of Trajan's Column. Built very nearly on a human scale, the fountain burbles invitingly, and deceptively so; the four rivers it celebrates are far more dangerous than this gentle flow.

The fountain is extraordinarily powerful nonetheless. There, writes the cultural historian Simon Schama in *Landscape and Memory*, "all the currents of river mythology, Eastern and Western, Egyptian and Roman, pagan and Christian, flowed toward one great sacred stream," a stream that just happened to touch on the banks of the Holy See.

The rivers—the Nile, Danube, Ganges, and Plate—describe the world of Bernini's time, a world rich in possibilities, a world fated for destruction and regeneration. Beyond that world, when the sluices of the fountain opened in 1652, lay only dragons, as the cartographers of old indicated on their maps. Three and a half centuries later, we are still limning their domain, still seeking just where those dragons are hiding, biding their time.

Whenever I go to Rome, I make first for the Fountain of the Four Rivers. Standing among the antivivisectionists and post-Communists there in the Old Ghetto, I try to allow myself the leisure of seeing the world as Bernini did, the pleasure of imagining a world in which every contour is known and classifiable. The world is not like that, of course. And my own world is more circumscribed still: it is a tiny slice of the known but unknowable world. It lies within the bounds of the four rivers of the Greater Southwest—the Colorado, the Gila, the Rio Grande, the Sonora—in the heart of the arid place that nineteenth-century cartographers called the Great American Desert. They are but four of the three thousand rivers on this gentle planet born of Oceanus and Tethys, children whose offspring are Metis, wisdom, and Tyche, fate. Beyond them lie dragons. Or perhaps Gila monsters.

It is more than world enough, more world than anyone can know in a thousand lifetimes. It is, for all purposes, *the* world.

II

Within the banks of those four ancient, dusky rivers lies a homeland.

In the opening pages of *A Portrait of the Artist as a Young Man*, James Joyce's Stephen Dedalus, wondering at his place in the world, records his address in the flyleaf of a geography primer:

Class of Elements
Clongowes Wood College
Sallins
County Kildare
Ireland
Europe
The World
The Universe

Joyce wrote at a time when the enormousness of the universe was just becoming known, a time when parsecs and light-years were a language unknown to all but a few and unimagined even by Joyce himself, a time when, conversely, the world was just beginning to shrink. We take all these things for granted nowadays, impatient in such matters. But it is healthy to consider the land with Dedalus's—and Bernini's—wide-eyed reverence, healthy to locate with his hushed wonder a place within this circuit of rivers: in my case, tracing backward, descending, from the huge cold Pacific Ocean into the narrow whaleroad of the Gulf of

California, up the Colorado, the Gila, the Santa Cruz to the Rillito to the thin pebbled channel that guides rainwater from the roof of my house across a windswept, snaggled desert garden all the way back to the shores of Japan.

III

Drawing on paleontology, climatology, ethology, and other disciplines, scientists have lately been speculating about what the ancestral homeland of humankind might have looked like. Environmental psychologists find the answer in the habitat in which most people would dwell if given free choice: a place atop a low hill, close to flowing water, with open grasslands and nearby forests of high-crowned and many-branched trees. This habitat, the biologist E. O. Wilson writes, corresponds almost exactly to the savannas of Africa a million and more years ago, when the first humans emerged.

It also corresponds to certain spots along the middle waters of the Black, the Hassayampa, the Verde, and the Mayo Rivers. I will not say just where, believing that part of the pleasure of making them a homeland, an essential component of one's private medicine bundle, is the search for them, and perhaps even the subsequent concealment.

But it may be enough to say that where home and homeland unite lies something like paradise.

IV

The Northern Irish poet Michael Longley once spent a long evening with me talking of many things: the *Odyssey*, the poetry of the Scottish nationalist Hugh MacDiarmid, the shape of coastlines and the contours of dreams. We talked, too, of the usefulness of list making as a poetic device, one that dates at least to the Homeric epics. In his elegy "The Ice-Cream Man" Longley lists the names of twenty-one wild grasses and wildflowers from the Burren, the rocky wilderness of County Clare, in homage to a murdered man who sold twenty-one flavors of ice cream from a Belfast storefront. Their names ring like church bells: valerian, loosestrife, twayblade, angelica, mountain avens, stitchwort.

The best way to know a place in its totality is to know the things it contains. To know those things means making lists, wondrous rosters full of surprises, delights, and especially interrogatives, in notebooks that grow into magical luminous epics with every increase in local knowledge. You will find that poetry at work in the pages of Thomas Jefferson's *Notes on the State of Virginia*, in the lyrics of Mary Oliver, in Hugh MacDiarmid's majestic poem "On a Raised Beach," perhaps the greatest hymn ever written to the English language, if not to the natural world.

"Listings," William Kittredge writes, truly, "are attempts to make existence whole and holy in the naming." Michael Longley sings the Burren into being. My multidecade research project, to borrow Ed Sanders's useful phrase, has been to know something

of this land of four rivers, to make a Homeric catalog of what it contains and conceals, to guess out its
soil series and oromorphology, to know where its
waters come from and where they go.

The names ring, too, in the fine poetry inherent in
the mere act of naming: feldspar and chalcedony,
andesite and larkspur, *Felis concolor* and columbine,
asphodel and salix, velvet ash and onza, cholla and
Canis lupus mogollonensis, gadts'agi, 'ida' dilko,
Spanish bayonet.

"Whole sight: or all the rest is desolation," writes
John Fowles. These are things we must carry in this
land if we are ever to see it clearly: names, memories
of names, dreams of names.

Clarity of vision is a hard habit to acquire. In 1764
the Jesuit Juan Nentvig, Silesian by birth, toured
New Spain, this land of four rivers, to report on conditions after a series of Indian uprisings. "Many of
the so-called rivers of this province," he wrote, "are
actually mediocre streams." Used to the broad
sweeping rivers of the Central European Plain, he
was impressed only by the Colorado. "Nothing is
certain of its source," he remarked, "but from its
grandeur, breadth and depth, capable of admitting
vessels of no mean dimensions, one deduces that
its sources must be far"—as far away, he guessed, as
the country of the Mandan Sioux, far up on the
Missouri.

He was beginning to see, but Nentvig's apparent
scorn for the land kept him from appreciating the
grandeur of water in the slimmest rivulet, the bearer

of water from Sonora to the shores of far-off nations, the bearer of rain from this dusty garden to
the shores of Japan.

V

Rivers are properly the province of birds, and birds
are their proper rulers. Once, at dawn along a slender tributary of the Colorado, the Bill Williams
River of northwestern Arizona, a turkey vulture
stared me down, rising up on its talons and spreading its wings vampirelike to chase me away from its
store of water, the domain of *Cathartes aura.*

To know a place is to know its languages, and the
language of rivers is the language of birds. The call
of a cactus wren speaks more of deserts than a shelf
full of hydrology reports. Beyond it lie dragons.

VI

Flowing water makes us sane. In India, madmen are
tied to tall trees beside rivers and left there to con-
template the passing stream. Regardless of what an
American clinical psychologist might say of this
regime, I am inclined to think that it works. You do
not often read of Indian mass murderers, after all, at
least on nothing like the scale that fuels our own
newspapers.

Let them carry away all pestilences, goes a Nepali
shamanic chant: Let the four rivers carry them away.

VII

Some people collect postage stamps, others English motorcycles. I collect rivers. I have seen many, and so here is another list: the Thames, the Potomac, the Danube, the Mississippi, the Tiber, the Lerma, the Rhine, the Black Warrior, the Seine, the Hudson, the Yangtze, the Huang Po. (Has there ever been a tribe to bestow an ugly name upon a river? Their appellations sing. Even Dry Beaver Creek, in central Arizona, has its charm.)

But—and here is the collector's impulse at work, the impulse that leads to empires and libraries alike—there are countless more rivers that I have never seen. I hope to stand alongside them one day: the Lena, the Brahmaputra, the Blue Nile, the Mackenzie, the Volga, the Amazon, the Ganges, the Amur, the Oxus. And the Gila, the Sonora, the Colorado, the Rio Grande, the rivers that once ran abundantly through this desert, bounding and defining the province where I live. These I long to see in their true form one day.

You cannot help but think of water when summer comes to the desert. It is a weird, trying season, punctuated only by small changes in the intense heat of day, when the dawn brings a wall of glaring white light on the land, washing out its colors, when human and animal life slow to torpor until night has fallen. Those foolish enough to stay willingly in the desert in summertime eat bushels of fruit, seek shade and breezes, and keep abundant liquids within easy reach, knowing only that the next six months will bring the same heat, day after day, hour after hour. One dares not read Raymond Chandler's short story "Red Wind" for fear that this time, yes, the heat will prove too much for the murderer within.

But the season brings rain as well, half the rain that will fall each year on the beautiful, generous Sonoran Desert, ten inches or so of water that you can almost hear the saguaros and Gila monsters lap up. The lightning-lashed rise of an afternoon storm in July is enough to give birth to a new theology, as deserts have bred the world's great faiths. It is a fine and oppressive time. It makes one think of water, of the wide and open sea.

And so, as every summer, I have been thinking of rivers. I have been thinking of the rivers I have seen, more of the ones I have not. And I have been thinking how strange it is that we should know so many of our rivers, we desert rats, only by their absence, only as tiny blue scratches, separated by ellipses, on highway maps, in the cartographic code for the dead. The desiccated beds of those once great rivers, spanned by unsteady bridges, mock their intended function, carrying runoff from the heavens only a few days of the year, effluent from sewage-treatment plants with greater regularity. For the rest of the year, bone-dry, they serve as drag strips for three-wheeled recreational vehicles and other criminalities, as dumping grounds for unwanted mattresses and pets, for defaulting cocaine consumers. They are rivers in name only, an insult to the theory and practice of flowing water.

Not so many years ago, those rivers streamed perennially. Barges followed their courses through the desert. Animals and people came to their deep pools to swim and drink, to escape the summer's heat and glare. Dense forests, rich with birds, lined the banks, and the riparian grasses grew so high, early observers wrote, that a man on horseback could ride through them without being seen. The rivers served as highways for animal species who moved from one mountain chain to another, seeding the alpine islands with their kind, and who are rarely seen now: the cougar, the grizzly bear, the jaguar, the Mexican gray wolf. All a budding naturalist had to do was find a tree stump and enjoy the passing show.

The people of Tucson once spoke of the Santa Cruz, our local watercourse, as the river, *el río*. It served as the natural center for a city that now lacks any axis, that now sprawls from one end of a thirty-mile-wide valley to the other, without anchorage or pivot. Its banks sported groves of shade trees—walnut, mesquite, cottonwood, oak—and gazebos filled with brass bands and mariachis, rope swings and diving boards, green sweeping lawns, dancing bears whose ghosts now haunt the old barrios. Western Tucson took on the aspect, for a generation or two, of a frontier Tuileries, a back-country Battersea Park. To look at the old pictures, you'd think it were another world entirely.

It was, and between it and us lie dragons.

But that was years ago, far beyond the memories of all but the very old, long before this desert city had grown to shelter more than half a million people. Each of them uses a hundred gallons of water a day, and so the river has been bled dry. Tucson now takes from its aquifer, an ancient underground river that once fed the surface streams, anywhere from four to ten times the amount of water that is recharged naturally through rainfall. Such an imbalance cannot continue indefinitely, of course, and some hydrologists have estimated that the city has less than thirty years before it exhausts the available water resources of the entire region.

Where the four rivers once flowed endlessly, mining and stock raising altered the face of the land through massive soil erosion and watershed degradation. The scars will not heal for millennia. Agricultural and political promoters declared to an eager world that the dry desert was a fine place to grow such wetland crops as oranges, pecans, and cotton. Legislators and other prophets of the short term convinced postwar America that earthly happiness was to be found in the fragile Sunbelt, far from snow and rust and the rotting leaves of autumn. Four of the five C's officially proclaimed as the basis of Arizona's well being—cattle, cotton, copper, citrus, and climate—condemned our rivers to extinction.

Now a new river, this one of human artifice, makes its way across the desert, zigzagging through the lava chaos and the ancient cactus forest, hacked from the parched ground and dropped out of the wombs of giant paving machines: the Central Arizona Canal. After fifty years of congressional battles for its funding, the canal's supporters are pleased to call the Central Arizona Project, its progenitor, the greatest engineering feat since the pharaohs' pyramids. Never mind that the canal hastens the death of the terminally ill Colorado River, from which it draws its water, a stream exhausted by the voracious demands of Los Angeles, Las Vegas, the Imperial Valley. Damn the lessons of history: the Sumerians may have destroyed their civilization by overdrafting the Euphrates River, but, well, things were different then. Never mind that the canal, by diverting water from the Colorado, will continue to turn the beautiful Sonoran delta, where the river once thundered into the sea to capsize incautious ships, into a silt-choked mudflat. Never mind that it will destroy a fragile desert ecosystem, that it will sever the migration routes of dozens of endangered terrestrial species: the new river will bring millions more inhabitants into the desert, a dream come true for the politicians and developers who roam the American landscape, insisting that limitless growth is good for us one and all. (Edward Abbey rightly countered, "Growth for its own sake is the ideology of the cancer cell.")

It is not much of a river. The cement-lined canal, an even uglier version, if it can be credited, of the Los Angeles River, has not blossomed with picnic grounds and bandstands. It has not given rise to groves of towering cottonwoods and willows. Instead, hundreds of miles of chain-link fence has sprouted from the earth, studded with one "No Swimming" sign after another, another instantly recognizable species of American public architecture of the late twentieth century. Southern Arizonans have not flocked to its banks in search of relief from the summer sun. The new river has not replaced the old city's riparian commons. It has not made us prosperous. Certainly it has not made us happy, made us sane, as flowing rivers do.

Perhaps it is a function of age, but I am becoming less and less patient with the notion that humans should be able to see rivers as challenges, as things to be conquered. Our grasp is just too small, and it is time that we recognized that, reduced the debate to the practical matters of daily life. We tame horses not to subdue their spirits but to ride them. We tame rivers not to dominate nature but to make money. Now that we are coming to see, at least in the desert Southwest, that our economies are marginal, rivers may have a chance to flourish simply because it is no longer cost-effective to try to bend them to our bidding.

And so to bring back the old rivers is not an impossibility; to declare that time cannot be reversed is mere dogma. (Of course it can. Is time not a wheel? Reverse all engines.) But to regain the Sonora, the Gila, the Colorado, the San Pedro—residents of any other town west of the Hundredth Meridian need only substitute appropriate names for the rivers they have lost—will require an absolute change in the politics and economics of the desert, toward a sustainable ethic that recognizes water as the best of all clean industries, the best, as Herakleitos says, of all things.

A free-flowing river in the heart of the desert, gleaming like an emerald in the heat of summer, perennial, available to everyone: the thought sweetens a thousand dreams.

Riverrun.

VIII

An Anglo anthropologist once asked a Hopi why so many of his people's songs were about rain. The Hopi replied, Because water is so scarce, of course. Is that why so many of your songs are about love?

All life is animated water, the Russian scientist Vladimir Vernadsky has told us. And our body, says Novalis, is a molded river.

Animated water, water of love, molded rivers: Imagination is what we have. And imagination is what we are left with. It is one of the few things that cannot be stripped away from us.

Imagine rivers. Imagine the four rivers: riverrun.

I am haunted by possibilities of resurrection in this chewed-up world, the possibilities of bringing again to life what has been destroyed: the Library of Alexandria (and Jorge Luis Borges's Library of Babel), the Aral Sea, thousands of lost species, languages, peoples.

And that is what remains for us to imagine: how to make that resurrection, that new renaissance, possible.

The four rivers: riverrun.

Oasis

In the three decades I have lived in Arizona, I have become something of a collector of oases and rivers. This has been useful knowledge for survival, and acquiring it has led me into some unexpectedly beautiful corners of this dry state.

One of the most beautiful no longer exists. It lay along the Gila River just outside the small copper-mining town of Winkelman, where a dense thicket of cottonwood, velvet ash, and willow trees crowded a low, gray-brown sandstone cliff to shut out the sun. It was dark enough in that glade that ferns and soft grasses could grow, cool enough to make even the hottest summer day in that perpetually hot part of Arizona bearable. Between this small riverside forest and the cliff stood the narrow Gila, quiet after a run through a boulder-choked canyon just upstream, a canyon that eventually fed out to the spillway of Coolidge Dam.

Within this sanctuary, which the people of Winkelman used as an unofficial but still popular municipal park, it was possible to imagine that we lived in a different time, and certainly a greener place, a time when industrial civilization had not yet finished the job of killing Arizona's rivers. Over the years I spent many hours there, taking soda breaks on the way from Tucson to the Mogollon Rim, watching birds, working over notes for a book I was writing about the natural and human history of the Gila.

At that narrow bend of the river lived an old Mexican American woman, whose small frame house lay perhaps fifteen yards from the stream, surrounded by mesquite trees in whose branches she had hung dozens of hummingbird feeders. Those feeders drew hundreds of hummingbirds from the surrounding desert, so many of them that approaching her house you would swear you were entering a great beehive filled with flashing creatures whose song went *zún-zún, zún-zún*.

In this oasis both natural and human-made, pride of ownership went foremost to those rainbow-hued Anna's, Costa's, calliope, broad-tailed, and rufous hummingbirds that sheltered here, and then to the squadrons of tanagers, kingfishers, jays, merlins, and eagles who watched over the proceedings and occasionally snacked on the slower of the hummers.

An interloper with no claim but of affection on the place, I suppose it met all my standards of paradise, with its cool water, its grasses, flowers, and trees, its abundant wildlife.

I suspect it met the hummingbirds' idea of paradise, too. Had we some way of asking, I would want to know for certain.

But for this oasis, questions would come too late: all but dead after generations of damming and overuse, the Gila River danced a Ghost Dance and came to life with a vengeance for a few weeks in 1993, churning over the Coolidge Dam upstream, roaring through Winkelman, gnawing everything in its path. What the 1993 floods did not take away, those of 1999, which turned out to be an uncommonly wet year, swept downstream. Bits and pieces of the little town now decorate the artificial waterways of Phoenix.

The doña's house and hummingbird feeders disappeared in a wall of water. So did most of the trees that lined that small kink in the river's course. Where they once stood is now a wide, stony beach, and on that beach now loll herds of cattle—a desert river's worst enemy, and a reminder, if we needed one, that impermanence and destruction are our lot in the world.

Where the old woman went I do not know. I hope she has helped make another oasis somewhere else in the desert to give weary travelers a little pleasure. The world she helped make before is gone.

But not entirely, for just a couple of days ago I watched hummingbirds come to the Gila, not in phalanxes as before but in twos and threes, to reclaim this slender ribbon of water.

Harboring a few Ghost Dance sentiments of my own, I know that as long as those birds grace our rivers, there is hope for this flood-battered, strip-mined corner of the world yet.

The Language of Hawks

That which happens to men also happens to animals; and one thing happens to them both: as one dies so dies the other, for they share the same breath; and man has no preeminence above an animal: for all is vanity. All go to one place; all are made of dust, and all return to dust again.

*—*Ecclesiastes

T hey come in with the setting sun, sweeping the treeline, gliding on the bumpy thermals over the grass-bare corral, a sortie returning from some ancient mission. One lands on the lightning-shattered limb of a cypress. Another takes a spot on a rotted wooden wheelbarrow. Still another finds a roost on the shake roof of an old barn. One by one the hawks settle over the house and gardens, standing guard over its perimeters. From time to time they issue the "deep, descending ARR," as a guidebook says, that marks their cry of alarm.

Then, as if assured that all is well, they gather in the quickening twilight, together singing down the darkness until the quiet night falls.

Raptors are by nature solitary birds. They are given to coursing alone through the skies to take their prey, and to sitting alone to dine once they've caught it. You'll see them winging along cliffs and over river canyons, a golden eagle here, a merlin there, throughout the desert Southwest, almost always alone. But the Harris's hawk, *Parabuteo unicinctus,* is a proud exception. The most social of the North American raptors, Harris's hawks come together to nest, hunt, eat, and relax, forming crowded families of stern adults and rambunctious young who fill the air with shrill cries of RAAA RAAA RAAA, demanding food.

You'll find them in groups, these Harrises, resting atop telephone poles or circling over freshly mowed fields, anywhere from Argentina to South Texas. But you will find them nowhere more abundant than here in the southern Arizona desert, where, for reasons that scientists do not understand, they nest more densely and in greater numbers than anywhere else in their range.

I can guess, though. Watching the families of Harris's hawks that make their homes on our little ranch, which lies at the edge of a rapidly growing city, I suspect that their great numbers have something to do with the ease of taking prey in a place where bulldozers and dragchains expose so much wildlife to the elements. In few other places have humans been so diligently ripping apart the fabric of the land, big yellow machines serving as native beaters on a safari of massive scale, chasing up the rabbits, quail, wood rats, and snakes on which Harrises feed as a by-product of destruction. It is a devil's bargain: the machines come for the hawks, too, tearing down the trees and cacti in which they nest. And more: many hundreds of Harris's hawks are electrocuted each year on the unshielded power lines on which they like to sit. The ease of finding food in a growing metropolis is thus a calculated risk, one that the Harrises seem to have taken despite all the attendant perils, much like their human counterparts. The carnage is appalling.

On a winter's morning late last year, one Harris's hawk was having nothing of the too abundant electrical wires that crisscross the rural landscape beyond our home. Instead, she had taken a perch on a leafless elderberry trunk, where she methodically spread her flight feathers to dry in the thin sun, yawning lazily.

She was not alone. No more than ten inches away from the foot-tall hawk, on a neighboring branch, stood a female mockingbird, screaming up a storm as if to protest the hawk's very presence. Call her proximity to the predator brave or stupid, this particular representative of the species *Mimus polyglottos* was doing her all to live up to her name, which means "the mime of many voices." (That name is very well deserved. When I lived in downtown Tucson I was often awakened by the too sensitive burglar alarm of a nearby electronic-supply house. The owner eventually got around to fixing the alarm, but too late; in its place came an uncanny rendition of the alarm's squall by the mockingbird that lived happily in my chinaberry tree, terrorizing the neighborhood cats and loudly proclaiming its territorial boundaries.) On this winter's morning, the mockingbird squawked, cried, bawled, and fussed, all the while flashing her wings threateningly in an attempt to intimidate the hawk.

It did not work. The Harris's hawk merely gazed off in the middle distance, trying, it seems, to ignore both the mockingbird and a curious hummingbird that came fluttering by to see what the fuss was about and hovered over the scene, a neck-craner of the sky. The air filled with the mockingbird's screech, the hummingbird's whirr, and the hawk's stony silence. And so it went for a couple of hours, a standoff straight out of Sergio Leone's *The Good, the Bad and the Ugly,* with the hawk stoically enduring the mockingbird's dressing-down, the hummingbird docked in midair, ignoring the nearby cornucopia of flowers to keep track of the proceedings, and me crouching at the foot of the tree with camera and notebook and field guide in hand, trying to decipher what seemed to me to be decidedly uncharacteristic behavior on the part of all concerned.

I never did find out what the dispute was all about, but the controversy has endured. I have seen the mockingbird upbraid members of our resident family of Harrises on several occasions since. I have seen no evidence of the hawks' taking punitive action in turn, found no scattered mockingbird components in the great bonefield that lies below the hawks' favorite eating spot, a wind- and lightning-tortured salt cedar overlooking our neighbors' corral. All of which leads me to add another quality to my list of anthropomorphizing adjectives for the Harrises: they are not only sociable, friendly, and family-minded, but also extraordinarily patient, more patient than I could ever hope to be in similar circumstances.

Not speaking a word of hummingbird, I was at a loss watching the verbal battle of the birds: a drama had played out in a language I could not fathom. I felt somewhat as I had when, a few months earlier, stuck in a slow elevator in Beijing, I endured an argument between two men, a Russian and a Chinese, both quite drunk. I did not know quite enough of either of their tongues to know what their argument was about, but their body language suggested that it was not a matter of life and death. I relaxed, but was still grateful when the elevator doors finally opened to release me. As I left, the Russian turned to me and said, in good English, "I saw you walking on the Great Wall yesterday. You were talking with a Chinese woman. You talked to another Chinese woman in Tiananmen Square yesterday in the early morning after you practiced your Tai Chi." Very true, I said. Are you a spy? "Yes," he said, smiling brightly through the vodka haze. "But for which government? Hah!"

It is my turn to spy, and so I have been doing. In these last months I have made it a point to study the language of hawks and mockingbirds and hummers, trying to strip away sentimentality and wishful thinking to get at an understanding of the avian mind, at least as it manifests itself in these local moments of grace. Mostly I have been following the hawks around from tree to tree, watching as they scoop up rabbits and ground squirrels, listening to the beg-and-solicit calls of the young, the sharp warnings of the old. I like to think that I am not intruding, that the keening cries that meet me as I step off the porch in the morning are glad greetings, and not admonitions to stand clear. Yet after months of studying their behavior, I find that I know really little more about either hawks or mockingbirds—or hummingbirds, whose actions are really quite transparent—than I did before. Just when I think I've hit upon a syntactic rule in what Henry Thoreau called their *gramática parda,* or "tawny grammar," they go off and invent a maddening exception that defies all logic. Just when I think I've anticipated cause and effect, they wheel off skyward and do the unexpected. Their every action is a koan, a puzzle, the solution to which is, I suspect, a door into the universe.

I am sorry to say that in my deciphering of this puzzle, the standard reference books have not been of much help—and for good reason. When I was studying for my graduate degree in linguistics twenty-odd years ago, a self-evident canard was accepted as iron law: Only human beings have language. Language, in the academic view, was narrowly defined as an open-ended system of signs and sounds, one that could accommodate new situations—the introduction of fire, say, or the arrival of new predators, or the discovery that the juice of a particular flower was good to eat. Humans, the dogma held, can instantly generate new utterances in response to hitherto unencountered phenomena, countless variations on a theme, whereas animals are bound to what they innately know, so that a snow monkey could never relate to another snow monkey the pleasures, say, of scuba diving or the Sicilian defense, only of the virtues of washing a sandy bit of apple in a clear stream.

I doubted the scholars' insistence that humans held so special and unique an advantage over the animals, but I kept my beliefs to myself, silently hoping that a surge of interest in animal language and thought would wash the academicians' sins clean. Twenty years later, that has not yet happened. There have been many advances in the study of both human languages and animal communication, but almost none of the point at which they meet, and we have not appreciably broadened our formal definitions of what constitutes language and who is entitled to have it. That work remains for future generations of scholars, who will likely look back on our time and wonder at our small-mindedness. I think here of what a doctor friend is fond of observing: that even the most advanced therapeutic and interventionist techniques of today's medicine will seem hopelessly barbaric a few years down the road. The standard references do not admit to such weakness. Instead, they insist, simply and adamantly, that animals have no language.

For many years, influenced by the great writer-philosopher Elias Canetti, who found time in the midst of World War II to ask what original sin the animals had ever committed, I have held a contrary view to that of the textbooks: that animals know very well how to talk to one another, but have the good sense to keep their opinions safe from human ears. It has long seemed self-evident to me that, despite what the professors have to say about the matter, animals communicate, inventively and continually and constantly. In this field of hawks, in the real-world setting of this small Arizona ranch, a place in which theory daily gives way to practice as I negotiate my way among a menagerie that numbers not only a full complement of Harris's hawks, mockingbirds, and hummingbirds but also horses, coyotes, camels, mules, lizards, several varieties of venomous and nonvenomous snakes, and a timber wolf, I have been testing that view daily.

It is a haphazard laboratory, but it affords me ample opportunities to watch closely as the animals speak to one another, and to me. And as I have watched, I have tried to sound out hawkish phonemes, filled small notebooks with observations, made stabs at collecting dictionaries, marking this place with words as our wolf would with urine, making these few acres the scene for what the poet Ed Sanders calls, luminously, a "multidecade research project"—namely, an understanding of my home ground and of the beings that share it. That project is just beginning, and others are carrying it out as well, students of language and thought around the world. We have much material to work with. It is all around us. We know much more about animal communication than we think we do, know it in our bones. When a hawk calls, we turn to see why. When a dog barks, we pay it heed. Underlying our own language is that *gramática parda,* that tawny grammar. The language of our animal fellows lies hidden—and not too deeply—in our every word.

Hundreds of thousands of years ago, when modern humans began to branch off from their primate kin, they developed a means of calling to one another not in the grunting language of their ape cousins but in the language of birds, in song. *Homo sapiens,* as the anthropologist Frank Livingstone notes, is the only

primate that can sing. And, he continues, "since singing is a simpler system than speech, with only pitch
as a distinguishing feature, I suggest that he could
sing long before he could talk and that singing was
in fact a prerequisite to speech and hence language."
And why the language of birds, and not of crickets or
leopards? Perhaps, it does not seem too far-fetched to
say, because our shrewlike distant ancestors developed their intelligence in the arboreal world of the
birds, so that our pop songs and Gregorian chants
and arias are tracks of memory stretching back
millions of years into the past. "Song is Being," wrote
Rainer Maria Rilke, more truly perhaps than even he
knew: our song, our human language, recapitulates
its origin with every syllable.

Underlying our awareness of the world, although
we are not usually conscious of it, is another awareness: that of ourselves as animals, if animals with the
gift of an unusually open-ended code of communication. This unusual advantage came about because
our distant ancestors recognized their kinship with
the animals, paid attention to the paths of birds, to
the tracks of ruminants and their predators, to the
movements of snakes and dragonflies. Movement is
mind: what humans are best at, of all the things
that we can do, is constructing, describing, and
refining complex sequences of motion—a ballet,
the pass of a soccer ball, the ascent of a rock wall—
before performing those motions themselves.
Cognitive scientists suggest that this ability is the

central distinguishing factor of human intelligence: not the ability to speak but the ability to imagine, to consider possibilities, to map the future.

Can a hawk see its flight in its mind before it takes to the air? Can a mockingbird foresee chains of cause and effect when it presumes to correct a larger bird of prey? We know that ants and wolves alike form mental maps of the territories they traverse. We know that birds communicate real information in song. What we do not know, and what we will never discover so long as it is presumed that only we have language, is whether a bird can sing a landscape into being in its mind, whether the air above us is as dense with songlines as the desert of Australia, whether the melodious calls of warblers and nightingales convey notions of time and space.

We know so little. We are not even sure what questions to ask.

Mine are simple. One is this: What do hawks know? Let us imagine: they know and discuss the freedom of the air, the feel of the wind smoothing their flight feathers, the shapes of rodents and insects scurrying before them. Another is this: What do mockingbirds have to talk about? In conversation, they may complain of obnoxious hawks and nosy humans. They may boast of their children's accomplishments. They may plot revolutions.

Let me say it again: animals do talk. They cry from the trees and the sky, call out from the earth, urging us to pay attention. Even the most doggedly dualistic thought, which has led to such a great gulf between humans and the natural world, makes some allowance for this possibility; René Descartes himself observed that humans differ from animals largely in the versatility of their behavior and language, and not in the mere possession of their ability to form sentences. And so the animals talk, not merely in their calls and croaks and cries but in our own language, in the birdsong of primates.

And they talk to us, gently but insistently, through an ancient vehicle: our literature.

In the stories we tell about them, animals talk about many things. We use them to take the place of humans, and in transparent ways: you have only to glance at George Orwell's *Animal Farm* to see the scowling face of Josef Stalin, have only to consider Saint Francis's wolf to see great warring states in battle array. Animals are the foils by which we deliver unpleasant news about our own behavior, as Aristotle noted of his contemporary Aesop, who defended a corrupt Corinthian politician by telling a story about a fox and a hedgehog. The hedgehog, taking pity on the flea-infested fox, asked whether he might remove the vermin with his quills. "No," the fox replied, "these fleas are full of blood, so they no longer bother me. If you take them off, fresh fleas will come." So, Aesop said to the jury, if this man is removed from office, a new one will come along and rob the city all over again. The jury was unappreciative, and sentenced Aesop to die for having spoken so plainly.

Odo of Helmark, a Norman writing around A.D. 1300, offers the same kind of critique of the ruling class in a story that plays on the fact that in French *duc* means "horned owl" as well as "duke":

A sparrowhawk caught a dove and devoured it. The other doves took council. To whom should they complain? "To the duke," said they. The duke was a bird with a big head and a bigger beak; to him the doves complained about the hawk who had killed their kinsman, and demanded justice. Having heard their complaint, the duke replied with a great clearing of the throat: "Clok." "How well he spoke!" said the doves, "surely he will make a dainty morsel of the hawk." The hawk came a second time and killed another dove. The rest ran to the duke and cried "Give us justice." He answered "Clok." The doves said "How sternly spoken! how just he is!" The hawk caught a third dove. The doves went a third time to the duke that he might hear their complaint, and he said "Clok." Hearing this they exclaimed, "Why is it he always says 'clok,' and never gives us justice? Let us go to his king and denounce him as a fool and a deceiver." That is why the doves and the other birds mob the owl whenever they catch sight of him, so that he never dares to fly out, except by night, for fear the birds might kill him. Just so, when poor men claim justice for their injuries from kings and great lords, these often reply, "We shall give it, we shall give it"; but they might as well say "clok," for they never give anything. For theirs are false promises, and their "Clok, clok," really means "Pay, pay," and you'll never get anything in return but "clok."

We are the guests of the animals in this world, subject to their guidance. Open any book of folklore from anywhere in the world, and you will find them as mentors. Our literatures, our tall tales, our mythologies are full of stories about animals, full of moralizing and speculation, full of the most outlandish exaggeration and the most profound sympathy. If we take the beginnings of literature to be the paintings that Neolithic peoples left on Old World cave walls, we will see that animals were our first concern as writers, as keepers of memory. In the same way, our alphabets evolved as a means of counting sheep—and camels, and bulls, and geese—the letterforms changing from pictograph to stylized symbol, but always carrying within them their origins in the description of the natural world: A as in Aardvark, Z as in Zebra.

But today we refuse to be guided. We repay the hospitality of the animals badly, blinded by Promethean knowledge. As Elias Canetti observed, vis-à-vis those people who exalted humans as manifestations of divine perfection, "It turns out that we are actually God's lowest creature, that is to say, God's executioner in his world." The mounting toll of our victims, of electrocuted hawks and shotgunned wolves, proves him sadly right.

Clok, says the horned owl, in the stupid arrogance of power. We live in a time when scientists are ever more rapidly finding ways to unlink humankind from the pesky fetters of natural selection and mortality, busily repealing the laws of nature. We live in a time grown intolerably lonely, a time without animals, a time in which we introduce distance on distance between ourselves and animals, who more and more figure in our lives only as symbols, as actors in television documentaries, or as test subjects in laboratories. We are ever farther from the angel land of Hungarian folklore, ever farther from that heaven in which, American Indian myths concur, animals and humans finally return to the original state of grace, one in which they share language and kinship.

That distance grows. And with it, we may never come to understand what the animals are saying to us, calling to us from all sides. We may never learn the languages of hawk and hummingbird, of cougar and bear. In a world in which humans can live forever and food can be made in laboratories, it will hardly matter; in a world in which humans imagine that the animals truly are voiceless, it will not matter what a hawk says to a hummingbird, any more than it matters what a stone says to the sky.

Gerbert of Aurillac, the great scholar and musician, had many enemies on his way to becoming Pope Sylvester II a thousand years ago almost to the day. Those foes accused him of devil worship, necromancy, and sorcery; but most damningly of all, they said, Gerbert had learned how to speak in the language of birds, had acquired the forbidden knowledge of the gods. Gerbert smilingly denied the charges of black magic. And as for learning the language of the birds, he said, I am only curious to hear what they have to say. Even if I knew every word of it, he continued, do you imagine that the birds would become mine to command?

The knowledge we have acquired is a terribly dangerous thing, very close indeed to that of the gods. It seeks to bind the world to laws of our own making, laws in which animals have had no representation. It seeks, as Plato warned in the *Theaetetus,* to capture every bird in the sky and lock it away in the cage of our minds.

That is not the sort of knowledge I am after. I share Gerbert of Aurillac's mere curiosity, stumbling around through patches of devil's claw and climbing over fallen tamarisk branches to catch the last trailing note of a hawk's call just to hear what it has to say about the world. If I have any hope beyond that, it is simply to temper arrogant certainty with a dose of imagining, to pick a few locks and let loose a few imprisoned birds, and to speak, if only for a syllable or two, for those whom we still imagine to be voiceless.

American Byzantium

It begins with the wind. The wind blows always, incessantly, in Las Vegas, apocalyptic and unsettling, stirring up the detritus of an unfinished desert civilization: cigarette butts, tumbleweeds, thirty-gallon trash bags, show passes, throwaway flyers for massage parlors and in-room escorts, and, not so long ago, astonishing quantities of radioactive fallout. The wind comes howling down across the valley from Charleston Peak, sweeping dust and debris before it, announcing its authority in a howling blast. There is no escaping it. Wherever you go in Las Vegas you hear its fierce undertone, a roar punctuating the demented whoop-whoop of slot machines paying off their load of coin, the ever-present police sirens, the babel of languages that careens like shrapnel off half-walls and handrails: Japanese, Arabic, Persian, Spanish, Middle American.

The heat of Las Vegas drives the standup comedians' jokes: It was 123 degrees when I flew in to Vegas this morning. I would have gone to the sun, but all the flights were booked.

But the wind is the true defining feature of this place, and wind leaves no monuments. Instead, it tears them down. And in the windy city of Las Vegas, a legion of workers is now busily erecting and dismantling and rebuilding one monument after another, constructing and deconstructing the future ruins of Republican civilization, among which the wind will one day play.

Where the wind rules there was once also water, generous springs of bubbling water that nourished the tallgrasses for which Las Vegas—"the meadows," in Spanish—earned its name. Those springs, most of them now disappeared, flowed into streams. And those streams flowed southward into a great river, which would join the sea, and thence the ocean. Had they had their sources just fifteen or so miles north, those streams, like all others in the Great Basin, would have disappeared into the alkali pans of the inland desert.

Those free-flowing waters were a rarity in the arid Southwest, and they were recognized as such. In antiquity, local Paiute medicine people maintain, the meadows offered a natural gathering place, a ceremonial site where powwows and trading fairs were held. (Those gatherings have recently been re-created in the form of the Paiute Snow Mountain powwow.) John Charles Frémont, the Western explorer, found the area to be full of Indians of various tribes when he stopped on May 3, 1844, and wrote of the place, "After a day's journey of 18 miles, in a northeasterly direction, we encamped in the midst of another very large basin, at a camping ground called *las vegas*—a term which the Spanish use to signify fertile or marshy plains, in contradiction to *llanos*, which they apply to dry and sterile plains."

Those fertile plains drew later visitors, later settlers. From 1855 to 1857, a colony of Mormon ranchers began a cattle operation at Las Vegas, which ended after the Mormon church dismantled many of its communitarian enterprises and settlements. Mormons later returned to the area, having remade their religion into a more perfectly capitalist concern, and they thrived quietly. In 1905, the Mormons and a handful of other inhabitants gathered at what is now the intersection of downtown's Main and Fremont Streets, near the recently completed railroad depot and the first casinos. Those residents were on hand to participate in the first Las Vegas Land Auction, the event that, at least in local history, marks the founding of Las Vegas as a city, just as endless real-estate transactions define it today.

Las Vegas grew slowly at first, a supply and watering station for trains and automobiles crossing the great desert from Los Angeles to Salt Lake City. Its lifeline became the Los Angeles Highway, also known as the Arrowhead Trail, the road Hunter

Thompson would so fatefully follow from the bat-infested confines of the Mojave. Another lifeline, as literal as the first, became Hoover Dam, built during the Depression as one of America's greatest public-works projects. Las Vegas benefited, then as now, from the water the huge dam brought to it. It benefited just as much from the army of dam builders who came to the small town each weekend, lured by the handful of casinos and brothels. (A few of those establishments still exist, tucked away among the technological splendors of what is now called the Fremont Street Experience, a dazzling light show for the tourist market, its soundtrack a set of gambling-related tunes like "Viva Las Vegas" and "Luck Be a Lady.") The dam builders were followed by World War II–era defense workers, soldiers, and airmen, many of whom liked the spacious desert and stayed after victory was declared in Europe and the Pacific. Their lot was easier with the advent of consumer air-conditioning, which made those 100-plus-degree days survivable, which made Las Vegas and the rest of the American West habitable.

Legal gambling and tolerated if not strictly legal prostitution were still mainstays in the little Mormon crossroads, and with a postwar boom fueling the sub-rosa economy, organized crime came to Las Vegas in the persons of Benjamin Siegel, Meyer Lansky, Gus Greenbaum, and other refugees from the East Coast. It has been said that these men and their colleagues were the true architects of Las Vegas, but I prefer to think that they simply rode an already rising wave, and in any event their contributions to the city, good and bad, are far smaller than has been supposed. Much more important to Las Vegas history are largely unknown figures like Wilbur Clark, the owner of the old Desert Inn, who operated pirate gambling ships off the coast of California until he realized one day that he could just as easily lure Angelenos into the desert for their recreation, and at smaller inconvenience to himself. (He was, it seems, tired of having to outrun the Coast Guard, whose officers would not be bribed.) It was Clark's great dream that the federal government retire its wartime debts by holding a national lottery, to be administered by none other than himself. He was prescient: two dozen states and countless Indian nations now hold lotteries of the kind Clark proposed, recapitulating old history—for the Jamestown Colony was financed by a London lottery until 1621, when the king deemed widespread gambling "an inconvenience, to the hinderance of multitudes of Our Subjects" and banned it.

The real tutelary spirit of the historic Las Vegas is an even more shadowy figure, a man who first realized the power attendant in merging, as he did, the worlds of business, government, and entertainment, and who thereby helped create the vast collective *panem et circenses* machine of our time. He is the manufacturer and sometime moviemaker Howard Hughes, who moved to Las Vegas for a time in the 1950s and who settled there permanently on Thanksgiving Eve 1966, in the penthouse of the Desert Inn. He did not last long in the city; on Thanksgiving Eve 1970 he moved away again, a paranoiac whose investments—especially the soon-to-be-bankrupt Landmark Casino—were a string of surprising failures.

When Hughes first moved to Las Vegas in the late 1950s, he largely disappeared from public view after having for years fueled the newspapers with reports of his amorous and financial exploits, from Jane Russell to the *Spruce Goose*. And when he did, he created a small media industry: Hughes sighting. Gossip columns, business monthlies, and even the normally staid *Wall Street Journal* were filled, from issue to issue, with news of unconfirmed surfacings, speculations on why the curious billionaire had quietly been buying out little companies at the fringes of American capitalism, rumors of his having died in a plane crash on the Orinoco or the Zambezi. And Hughes himself, who once craved public attention, knowingly fueled the media's infatuation, never coming out into the open to speak for himself, alternately raging and rejoicing at the image the press had given him precisely because he would not.

His reclusiveness did not extend, however, to public affairs. From his Desert Inn penthouse, Howard

Hughes exercised an enormous influence on the presidencies of Lyndon Johnson and Richard Milhous Nixon, whom he called "our boy in the White House," manipulating American politics with a studied secrecy. Michael Drosnin hits it squarely with his remark, in his 1985 book *Citizen Hughes,* that "the great secret that Howard Hughes kept hidden was not this or that scandal, not this payoff or that shady deal, but something far more sweeping and far more frightening—the true nature of power in America."

Hughes's hidden network of political influence might never have been known to the American public had not a group of burglars broken into Hughes's corporate headquarters, a vast warehouse on 7000 Romaine Boulevard in Los Angeles, on June 5, 1974. They found money there, and a great deal of it, but they also took something much more valuable: ten thousand pages of secret documents, including some three thousand in Hughes's own hand. The Federal Bureau of Investigation, despite a nationwide search, never recovered these papers. Michael Drosnin, a reporter for the *Washington Post,* did, through means that he has yet to make clear. His book, based on this primary evidence, spins a frightening tale of just how malignant Hughes was, and of how corrupt our politics have become.

Like many of his contemporaries in Hollywood, Hughes despised American democracy, and he freely exercised his contempt. Faced with a federal investigation into his business dealings, he wrote a memorandum to his aide, Robert Maheu, ordering him to blanket Capitol Hill with money until the problem went away. Hughes's payments were eagerly accepted, as he knew they would be, which only encouraged his contempt. He later wrote to Maheu,

> I dont aspire to be President, but I do want political strength. . . . I mean the kind of an organization so that we could never have to worry about a jerky little thing like this anti-trust problem—not in 100 years. . . . And I mean the kind of setup that, if we wanted to, we could put Gov. Laxalt in the White House in 1972 or 76. . . . It seems to me that the very people we need have just fallen smack into our hands.

Hughes got the people he wanted, although Nevada governor Paul Laxalt would not, as he hoped, become president. Of Lyndon Johnson, Hughes wrote, "we have a hard cash adult relationship," and Johnson, eager to match the description, awarded Hughes with an exclusive contract to supply the army with helicopters for the war in Vietnam. For his part, Richard Nixon gave Hughes any concession he asked for, fair trade for the hundreds of thousands of dollars Hughes poured into Nixon's 1972 reelection campaign fund. (Hughes's donations were laundered and used, among other purposes, to redecorate Nixon's California home, San Clemente.) Only the Kennedy family, grown rich a generation earlier on corruption of another kind, resisted Hughes's overtures, leading him to call them "a thorn that has been relentlessly shoved into my guts."

Howard Hughes did not always have his way, even under friendly presidential administrations, but his failures were of his own making. Desiring a national forum for his right-wing political views, he once tried to take over the American Broadcasting Corporation, failing to complete the purchase only because he would not leave his cavernlike bedroom high atop a Las Vegas hotel long enough to transfer ownership of the network in the Washington offices of the Federal Communications Commission. Hughes, a television addict who stayed up around the clock to watch one B movie after another, many of them pictures he had made, had reason to want ABC: in one of his memos to Maheu, he expressed his rage that on *The Dating Game,* a popular show, a white woman had been paired with a black man for an all-expenses-paid vacation to Rome. The woman was a light-skinned black, but that was not enough to convince Hughes that the liberal media were not secret agents of miscegenation.

Hughes was a committed racist. "Of all Hughes's phobias and obsessions," Drosnin writes, "few were more virulent than his fear and loathing of blacks." Immediately after Martin Luther King Jr. was assassinated in 1968, Governor Laxalt attempted to put into law a fair-housing act that he hoped would ease racial tension in Nevada, thereby averting the riots that had torn apart every major city in America. Enraged by what he perceived to be creeping communism, Hughes lobbied the Nevada legislature to ensure that Laxalt's bill would not pass, reasoning that blacks would leave the state if their situation were made uncomfortable enough. The bill failed, as it was almost certain to do in any event, given the state's archconservative politics and tiny minority population at the time. Laxalt left the governorship soon thereafter to move on to Washington as a United States senator.

The passage of a series of national civil-rights acts in the 1960s caused Hughes to exile himself from America in his final years, when it became apparent that even he could not buy the apartheid he wanted for his nation. He fled first to the Bahamas, then to Nicaragua, where he lived in absolute secrecy under the protection of his friend Anastasio Somoza until the great earthquake of December 23, 1972, which leveled Managua. Hughes had a paranoiac fear of germs and illness, and he demanded that all canned food served to him be handled with surgical gloves and washed bit by bit in germ-free bowls—and this after the cans themselves had been medically sterilized. Knowing that natural disasters breed disease, Hughes instantly quit Somoza, who seven years later would be toppled by the Sandinista revolution and soon thereafter assassinated with a shot from a well-aimed bazooka in Paraguay. Hughes took up hermitage in the skies, jetting back and forth between British Columbia, Europe, the Bahamas, and Mexico, never staying in one place long enough to attract attention. He died airborne on April 5, 1976, while traveling from Mexico City to Houston, Texas, the city of his birth. His aides, like the Chinese emperor Shi Huangdi's fearful retinue twenty-two centuries earlier, did all they could to hide the fallen ruler's death from the public.

He corrupted everyone he could reach, manipulated markets and presidencies, bought whatever and whomever he thought would serve his purposes. We have only begun to realize the extent of his activities, of Howard Hughes's sway over a nation and its rulers—and, for a time, over a windy desert city that did not make him its king but followed him nonetheless.

Howard Hughes is gone. His name lives on only in the occasional toponym, particularly Howard Hughes Parkway, which skirts the University of Nevada and the staggeringly busy McCarran International Airport. So, too, are gone most of the members of the Rat Pack, the lounge-act lushes who popularized Las Vegas as a swingers' paradise. So, too, are gone the waters that nourished the meadows.

And in their place has risen the new Las Vegas, the American Byzantium.

Je suis l'empire à la fin de la decadence.
—STÉPHANE MALLARMÉ

The future, writes Joan Didion in *Slouching Towards Bethlehem*, her fine book of essays about a New West now suddenly thirty years old, always looks good in this golden land "because no one remembers the past. Here is where the hot wind blows and the old ways do not seem relevant, the divorce rate is double the national average, and where one person in every thirty-eight lives in a trailer. Here is the last stop for all those who come from somewhere else, for all those who drifted away from the cold and the past and the old ways."

Didion needs to be updated a little: the rate of divorce and the number of Americans who live in trailers have both risen to startling heights, as have the sheer number of Americans who have drifted away from the cold Rustbelt and into the waiting arms of the sunny, amnesiac New West. She also needs to be corrected ever so slightly, for in several fundamental respects old patterns endure. One of them is this: Las Vegas has always been about addictions, addictions to land and open sky, addictions to sex and drugs, addictions to money and chance, all the artifices of eternity. It remains so today, in a time when once-shameful addictions have become matters for public confession, even sources of pride and of much sought-after street credibility.

These addictions are all-powerful, of course. I think here of the case of a seventy-eight-year-old man who, early in 1998, opened fire on a group of gamblers, wounding five of them. The shooter tried, without success, to escape, but his dependence on a walker prevented him from putting much ground between himself and the scene of the crime. For their parts, those who were shot continued to play the slots, refusing medical treatment until ordered to receive it.

"The essential American soul is hard, isolate, stoic, and a killer," wrote the British novelist D. H. Lawrence. It is all that and more: for the essential American soul thrives in equal parts on risk and security, on the thrill of taking chances—but only with a subsidy. "Those who live in the midst of democratic fluctuations have always before their eyes the image of chance," wrote Alexis de Tocqueville. "And they end by liking all undertakings in which chance plays a part." Those undertakings, cushioned and safety-netted, have devolved into forms of amusement, the chief products of late capitalism: abstractions all, abstractions fraught with anxiety, obsession, and addiction, from Game Boy to baccarat. Just stay out of the way of the bullets.

(Or else join in the shooting spree. One day, and perhaps not so long from now, or so my dark fantasy runs, I will receive news I would prefer not to hear: of impending financial ruin, perhaps, or some horrific legal action, or perhaps the advent of a terminal disease. And on that day I will make for the nearest scrap-arms dealer—there are countless of them in the stark solar deserts between my home and Las Vegas, camped in trailers, hiding from the sun under camo-tarp ramadas and surplus parachutes in the thorn-scrub forests—and buy an RPG or a bazooka, wind my way up U.S. 95 into Las Vegas, and make for the Mirage, where I will blast through the plate glass separating Siegfried and Roy's unfortunate, enslaved Siberian tigers from Republican civilization. The tigers will have a long-overdue feast; visitors to the Mirage will enjoy an unanticipated spectacle far more interesting than the usual exploding volcano and pirates on parade; and all concerned will test the balance between risk and security in a new game of chance.)

This much is clear: the Las Vegas of Howard Hughes, all cocktails and Lycra-clad waitresses turned out to pasture, the playground of the middle class, has given way to a different Vegas, one that recognizes, in defiance of official American ideology, that, yes, there are social classes here, and that the rich are different from you and me. Let us enshrine the formal date of that split as that of the destruction of the Dunes Hotel and Casino, October 27, 1993. The last of the great Rat Pack–era, middle-class hotels, the Dunes was dynamited before a huge crowd of onlookers, destruction as entertainment. Before it went the Hacienda and the

Sands, once-affordable places now bulldozed into the desert.

Yes, the class war has come to Las Vegas; no longer does everyone stand equal before the croupier. On one hand is the Las Vegas of the rich, whose center is now Shadow Valley, a golf course–cum–resort Xanadu for ultramoneyed gamblers, whose members are the high-stakes premium players who wager a million dollars on a hand of blackjack or a roll at the craps table. The management of Caesars Palace recently spent $13 million to equip just two suites for these high rollers, while at the MGM Grand Hotel a set of villas is being built for them at a cost of $700 million. Says Sandi Varvel, a public-relations executive whose job it is to market Las Vegas to the world, "With the opening of the Bellagio things went to a whole new level. When the hotel gets established it won't have a room for under two hundred dollars a night. Las Vegas used to be the home of the ninety-nine-cent shrimp cocktail and the dollar ninety-nine filet mignon, but no more. Now we've got four Wolfgang Puck restaurants. We're rivaling New York and Chicago for fine dining—but it's expensive, and it's not for everyone."

On the other hand is the mass-appeal, theme-park Vegas, the Las Vegas of family fun, Bermuda-shorts- and baseball-cap-clad broods locked in an aggregate adolescence, wandering from casino to casino as if taking in a Civil War battlefield or a grand tour of Europe. Not for them the Bellagio, said to be the world's swankiest hotel; these lumpen gamblers are confined to Circus Circus and Treasure Island, on the northern end of the Strip, toward the crumbling old downtown. Every class, every sub-class, now has its own casino, it seems, in a powerful example of niche marketing. Even convenience stores and filling stations here boast slot machines, and a Las Vegas firm has just announced a line of in-home one-armed bandits for the shut-in, or perhaps agoraphobic, market.

The first Byzantium was an imperial city at the crossroads of continents, class-stratified, a city that, with its empire, grew richer, more cultured, and weaker all at the same time. Its politics were an odd mix of religion, commerce, and entertainment, an oddly libertarian brew that proclaimed the need to depend on government but at the same time mis-trusted politicians, and for many good reasons. Byzantium is little remembered today save as a city, a culture, given to festal and sacral icons, the stuff of art-history courses and Sotheby's catalogs.

The icons of Las Vegas are not as obvious as Byzantium's, but they are there nonetheless, en-shrined in the casino, the interior oasis of troubled souls, pew after pew of slot machines before the altar of capital; not for nothing are casinos and churches alike kept dark and innocent of clocks, resulting in both spaciousness and timelessness, in a grand symbolic grammar. And what symbolism it is, a neon paradise that can be properly appreciated only at night. One has only to think of the grandfather of the *panem et circenses* casinos, the appropriately named Caesars Palace, built largely with financing from the Jimmy Hoffa–era, ill-fated Teamsters Union Central States Pension Fund, whose first owner, Jay Sarno, believed that the oval was the most restful of shapes, and perhaps the one thus most likely to relax the owners of wallets and purses enough to coax money from them. (He may have been right: several owners later, Caesars Palace remains one of the most consistently profitable casinos in Las Vegas.) Sarno therefore ordered that construction of the casino follow elaborate, egg-shaped patterns that can be only dimly discerned today, now that a Planet Hollywood and a shopping mall have been tacked on to the original structure. The egg, the world egg—a shape favored by Byzantine architects, too, who would have reveled in the splendor of Caesars Palace, with its eighteen fountains, its tons and tons of imported Mediterranean marble, its ersatz *Nike of Samothrace* (overlooking, as it happens, a Nike shoe store), all imparting authenticity to artifice. Those ancient architects would have also liked the MGM Grand Hotel, at this writing the largest in the world, and the architectural gigantism, and the endless trompe l'oeil adornment by which every improvement, every renovation, calls for a retaliatory spruce-up on the part of any neighboring building. Thus, whereas the newish Excalibur looks at this very moment a little run-down next to the fabulous and furious construction taking place at the nearby Luxor, it will almost certainly soon wear a new suit of armor, in homage to the doctrines of planned obsolescence and the short shelf-life of commodities in a world gone mad for them.

Las Vegas, city of icons, once considered to be a mere "spectacle suburb" of Los Angeles, has far surpassed the excesses of Disneyland and the junkier side of Hollywood. Edmund Wilson was right in his time to call Los Angeles the "great anti-cultural amusement-producing center" of America. Las Vegas is today just as vital as a center in the making of all our empty entertainments; were the film industry to be moved there, as "white flight" from Los Angeles may one day have it, Las Vegas would be the world's first utterly virtual metropolis.

Las Vegas is more than that. It is also a world city, the easternmost outpost of the Pacific Rim, a direct destination for airline flights from faraway continents. Now, in some Las Vegas restaurants the addition of *hoisin* sauce to a hamburger constitutes Pacific Rim cuisine, but I mean something deeper here; for I have just been traveling in China, where capitalism is being rebuilt anew on the other side of the Pacific Rim—China, Las Vegas's *semblable*, its reverse image in many ways. There corruption on the Howard Hughes scale has always been the rule, a corruption given new vigor in the booming economy; as one Communist Party member said to me, "The government has fun. They drink. They smoke. They go with girls. But they don't want the people to do this. Then they lose control of the people." And, said another party member, looking at the well-dressed young people on Shanghai's Nanjing Road, "In the seventies we had blue Mao suits. In the eighties we had business suits. In the nineties we have T-shirts."

He was right; T-shirts, the uniform of neoliberalism and Pax Coca-Cola, are everywhere, as ubiquitous on Nanjing Road as on Las Vegas Boulevard. But China is changing in more than just fashion. In a generation the standard of living has improved dramatically in almost every sector of society. There has been an immense reduction in poverty throughout the country. In the wake of the one-child revolution, me-first consumerism is rising, and, for the first time ever, there is plenty to consume, albeit at fearful cost to the environment. China's growth is astonishing; its economy is projected to surpass that of the United States and to become the world's largest by no later than 2020. Within the country, signs of this growth are everywhere. Old wood-and-brick neighborhoods in Beijing are being bulldozed away in the name of progress, displacing hundreds and thousands of people; one such neighborhood, not far from Tiananmen Square, is now being remade into a twenty-four-story megaplaza with shopping malls, health clubs, luxury condominiums, and four-star hotels.

In short, Beijing is becoming Las Vegas without casinos, another capital of twenty-first-century capitalism. And the casinos are not even necessary; when Beijing remakes the Forbidden City into a historical theme park, when the masses have open access to the demimonde of girls and alcohol and hitherto forbidden entertainments, the transformation of the western edge of the Pacific Rim into a mirror of the easternmost outpost will be as good as complete.

Las Vegas, crossroads of continents. My friend Lenadams Dorris, a native of the city who owns a hip little coffeehouse not far from the old downtown, is a rarity, an unapologetic admirer of all that is Las Vegas. He puts it just right: "Las Vegas is not really a city of the United States, but a city of the world," he says. "We have a zone of activity that is transnational; it is really irrelevant to us what our neighboring cities are doing. There was a terrible period in the late 1980s and early 1990s where Las Vegas was trying to paint itself as just another town, which is absurd. We're not just another town; we are the most spectacularly odd urban thing ever to happen on this planet. Let's revel in it, and if you can't revel in it, just shut up and let it revel in itself. We don't need to prove to the world that we are valid. They prove it to us every day, with their dollars." Not content to stop with that, Dorris even pictures a future Vegas as an emergent city-state along the Renaissance ideal, finally declaring its independence from the Nevada outback that it supports and allying itself with other such city-states and neo capitalist formations: the People's Republic of Santa Monica, perhaps, or, as in another of my fond dreams, the Holy Sonoran Empire.

Dorris celebrates the "real" Las Vegas, one that inarguably exists but is out of view of casual visitors, a Las Vegas of neatly clipped lawns and low crime rates, the Las Vegas of individual taxpayers and fast-food eateries. That Las Vegas is largely inaccessible to outsiders, to tourists who would not much be interested in it anyway. Certainly it is not promoted by the advertisers who tout the Mirage, the Bellagio, Circus Circus. A dead zone of decayed, abandoned buildings cordons off the vibrant Strip from the rest of the city, and few tourists venture beyond it. Beyond that dead zone of homeless shelters, blood banks, and rubble, beyond the Las Vegas equivalent of Byzantium's city wall, lies a different city entirely, one that stretches to the horizon, made up of a congeries of strip malls and walled suburbs. This Las Vegas illustrates an observation by the Indian economist Deepak Lal:

> In many ways, at the frontiers of the West . . . there is a re-turn to the Middle Ages, as "decent" citizens, irrespective

of race, increasingly live (or want to live) in gated communities or distant suburbs from which they commute to privately policed workplaces. The only danger lies in the public places they have to traverse in getting from home to work. These are infested with the modern versions of medieval highwaymen—muggers and carjackers. This growing failure of Western states to provide the most basic of public goods—guaranteeing their citizens' safety— is eroding their legitimacy, but it need not dissipate the economic vigor of the West. . . . This failure, however, will make the West a dangerous place in which to live.

A return to the Middle Ages, to Byzantium; those walled communities are a collection of city-states, republics of like-minded normality. Like Los Angeles, Las Vegas is growing, and to huge proportions. Even so, this world city is no city at all, no place with a real center; Las Vegans go to the Strip only to work. In place of any "real" Las Vegas, we have another reality altogether, that of the MGM Grand golden lion and a rising replica of the Eiffel Tower, that of carefully manufactured show.

"Evolution in Las Vegas is consistently toward more and bigger symbolism," write the architects Robert Venturi, Denise Scott Brown, and Steven Izenour in their now-classic 1977 study *Learning from Las Vegas*. "The Golden Nugget casino on Fremont Street was an orthodox decorated shed with big signs in the 1950s—essentially Main Street commercial, ugly and ordinary. However, by the 1960s it was all sign; there was hardly any building visible." Venturi and his colleagues, like Joan Didion, need to be updated, for Las Vegas is grown up now. The signs are smaller, the buildings more than those glorified sheds; instead, they are remarkably playful works of consumer art, icons with their own homegrown symbology. One has only to see the exceedingly odd New York, New York or the Luxor, which is becoming ever more plainly a monument of its own magnificence, to appreciate this point.

Las Vegas symbolism, always a national curiosity, is becoming an altogether strange thing, an artifact of self-reference: it encompasses the entire history of the planet, drawing on all times and places, the product of a global scavenger hunt, a bricolage of lincredible proportions, a paragon of what the architectural critic Reyner Banham called the "fantasticating tendency" of the Far West. That play of mixed histories produces strangely mixed results. Las Vegas is in many critical respects an utterly forward-looking city, but even if its current big-selling show is Mystère, a Cirque du Soleil piece that introduces conceptual and performance art to a mass audience, elsewhere it thrives on nostalgia; on a typical night early in 1998, the headline acts advertised on the Strip were Tom Jones, Mary Wells, David Cassidy, and George Carlin, time-warped in from the late 1960s. But so be it. Las Vegas is the world in miniature, a global *Wunderkammer*, encompassing Assyria and Manhattan, the Valley of Kings and the Valley of the Dolls, with all times, all cultures, all locations carted in as casino magnate Steve Wynn and his peers roam the world like modern-day Lord Elgins, transporting the ages to the new Byzantium, a city visible from far out in space.

Call it Worldland.

One of the stranger new entries in that theme park is Red Square, a restaurant inside the massive Mandalay Bay casino, at whose entrance stands a giant, headless statue of Vladimir Lenin. The interior is an amalgam of loot from the fallen nations of the Communist world: the central gold-and-crystal chandelier, for instance, is one of two taken from the Polish embassy in Moscow (the singer Michael Jackson owns the other one), and the proletarian art—mostly giant blood-red workers-of-the-world posters—decorating the restaurant's walls was scavenged from government flea markets throughout the former Soviet Union.

Red Square's interior has met with no objections, but the Lenin statue—manufactured in the United States, and originally with a massive head—did rile a few locals. "Some people were upset by it," says Sandi Varvel. "I guess they didn't understand that we won the Cold War. They probably don't understand the redistribution of wealth that goes on in the casinos, either."

Under the orders of Mandalay Bay's management, a team of welders swept down on Red Square in the middle of the night. When they were finished, the statue was without a head, which disappeared for a few weeks. "It turned up in a Las Vegas thrift shop," says Varvel, "and Red Square bought it back. They're going to encase it in ice and use it as a table in their vodka freezer."

A dangerous place, Las Vegas: dangerous for statues, dangerous for the ghosts of a failed past.

History repeats itself, said Karl Marx: first it comes as tragedy, then it replays as farce. A drive down the Las Vegas Strip reveals as much. We are replaying, everywhere in Western culture, the nineteenth-century tragedy of speculation, degradation, and accumulation, but now with very little in the way of actual production—which makes Las Vegas the model postindustrial center, the capital of the twenty-first century.

At the dawn of that new millennium, the world will be Las Vegas's: Howard Hughes's vision, enlarged, of a world in which politics, industry, and entertainment are one and the same. That world is already here, writes the Dutch scholar Wim Brockmans in his *A History of Power in Europe*:

> It is not the politicians who can now be considered the most effective interpreters of values and norms but the

hidden persuaders of capitalism who in the form of entertainment play on the aesthetic and emotional dimensions of the public. In this they have reached a degree of technical perfection which makes the propaganda campaigns of preachers in the thirteenth century, Jesuits in the seventeenth, nationalists in 1900, and bolshevists and nazis look paltry. What, then, is their message? Materialism, individualism, and competition, the core values of capitalism. Other values such as democracy, the rights of man and pacifism are put second by the capitalist entrepreneur and in practice desecrated daily whenever that improves his profit.

Brockmans is right. The world is turning ever more to entertainment as a way of fending off reality, learning the core values of capitalism in the process and paying for the privilege. And as it does, Las Vegas, or something very much like it, will be replicated around the planet in satellite cities in places like, well, China. This is not so far-fetched, for the twenty-first-century economy is likely to involve mass entertainment and games of chance on a scale without twentieth-century precedent. As a University of Nevada, Las Vegas, economist said recently, "I can't think of anything that gives as much hope for general social development, employment, economic development, health, and education as gaming operations." He was speaking of America's Indian reservations, but the rest of the Third World—and the Second, and the First—is fair game, too.

The world as casino: welcome to the millennium.

For now, there is but one Las Vegas. And in this aoristic city, the only real curiosities are the unbelievers and the documentarians, the filmmakers with their obligatory casino-lights-on-a-polished-car-hood cautionary tales, the doubting journalists. Swallow fire on Las Vegas Boulevard and you will be passed by; produce a notebook or a camera and you will draw onlookers outside a casino, security guards within—for Hunter Thompson's "don't burn the locals" rule, so often violated throughout the narrative of his *Fear and Loathing in Las Vegas,* has transmuted into "as long as it doesn't threaten the bottom line," which cameras and notebooks surely can do.

I think in this instance of a cold February night when the photographer Virgil Hancock and I went out to behold—and that is the word—the newly installed golden lion at the MGM Grand Hotel, an imperial symbol overlooking the city's largest intersection. Buffeted by an aggressively icy wind, we set to work: Virgil began making images with his zimpossible-to-conceal eight-by-ten camera, while I retreated to a corner and began taking notes on the passing scene. A tourist approached to ask what I was writing about. You, I replied.

I was not being supercilious. There, in the center of the world city, I was writing about him, and about the countless other tourists who stood gazing at the fabulous sights of the Strip, and about all of us at the dawn of the millennium.

"Your future begins here." So reads a billboard on the outskirts of Las Vegas, proclaiming the world city's message to its waiting empire. Your future begins here, here in the place of wind-eroded blue angels and boarded-up shops, here in a city that promises all manner of instant gratification and rewards believers with anxiety and loss: the hallmarks of late capitalism, all served up in spades.

Yes, the sign says, "Your future begins here." But it is worth remarking in the face of such optimism, as the poet Wallace Stevens did, that "Incessant new beginnings lead to sterility." For all its flash and glitter, for all its comfortable new developments stretching off to the horizon, for all its obvious wealth, Las Vegas is a sterile place, a world city of pastiche and pose, its very culture a commodity. In the end, this new American Byzantium resembles nothing so much as a wax museum.

Other signs tell other stories of Las Vegas, "Of what is past, or passing, or to come," to use the words of William Butler Yeats, that chronicler of the first Byzantium. "Drugs and prostitution prohibited." "300,000 couples happily married here." "You're a guaranteed winner." "Instant cash." "Homes for real families." "Where winners belong." "Cash a check here and get free Pepsi." "Totally nude review." "Life the life. Love the price." "Organized living. Get into it." "Global power for America." "Elvis slept here." "As real as it gets." And, of course, "No exit."

On the Strip, in the dead center, in the far-flung boomburbs, the rise and fall of Western civilization is recapitulated daily, and tragedy and farce freely combine.

As real as it gets, indeed.

Addiction, accumulation, sociopathy, dissimulation: Las Vegas, a cheap holiday in other people's misery, a tour of a place that thrives on and sells nothing but artful abstractions and hollow promises, the true icons of late capitalism. It is harder and harder to cut through the Potemkin village of our time to unveil what lies behind it, the enduring constants of this place: sun, water, and the wind that will one day erase any sign that we were here.

The future begins with them, and it begins here.

The Imaginary Atlas

Southern Utah is scorchingly hot in the summertime: good weather for rattlesnakes, poor weather for traveling in an automobile without air conditioning. And although the Mormon residents of that state—the only one in the Union to have been founded on a novel, as some wag remarked long ago—would not wish to see the thirst brought on by native heat thus slaked, one fine blazing summer afternoon on the road to nowhere, I stopped in Mount Carmel, once a lovely green town and now just another southwestern strip mall, for a cold beer with which to combat the elements. I found one, too, for even alcohol-shy Mount Carmel lies within the *oikoumené*, the habitable world of the Homeric poems, distinguished by the things of civilization.

I found three types of beer to choose from in the town's one restaurant, famous for its "Ho-Made pies." The selections were chalked up emphatically, in tall letters, on a plywood board over the cashier's stand:

> *Domestic beer   75¢*
> *Imported beer $1.25*
> *Eastern beer $1.75*

A rich geography of meaning underlies that sign, a sign that speaks volumes about how little desert towns see themselves in relation to the greener world beyond. The American East stands as terra incognita, alien from the familiar and the domestic, which in this instance meant the soapy offerings of the Adolph Coors brewery in Golden, Colorado, a short hop over the Rocky Mountains. The East is a land beyond the pale, more exotic even than those places from which silk and cinnabar must be imported. The Carmelite beer distinction, it seemed to me then, was rather like the map of Idrisi, made by the Arabian geographer for King Roger of Sicily in 1154, in which Tunisia—and, of course, Sicily—loomed preternaturally large while greater Russia and al Sind, or India, were but specks off the path of the Silk Route. The arc of the meridian and the pearlike figure of the revolving planet are well known, but the world they encompass stands scarcely imagined. As it well might be, for the East as Mormon Utahns remember it is a place of prophecy and oppression, far from the promised land of Zion.

The East Coast has its own version of Utahn insularity: Saul Steinberg's great, famous cover for the *New Yorker* is its talisman, a sketch in which New York is America, allowing for a bump off in the background to symbolize Pike's Peak and, far away, a tiny bridge to remind us of the existence of the Golden Gate. Every region and nation throws up borders, ideological or ethnic or cultural, from the Berlin Wall to the billboard that, in my childhood, greeted travelers along U.S. 95 as it entered Georgia—"This is Klan Kountry"—and the placard that even today hangs on the border turnstile at Naco, Mexico: *"No se admiten jipis."* No hippies allowed.

How are we to know those borders and the expectations they proclaim? How are we to comprehend the manifold divisions of the world in space and time? I read recently a magazine piece headlined, "Mongolia is struggling to come into the twentieth century," suggesting hopefully that the disastrous time which we inhabit ought somehow to be the omnicultural standard of choice, but also confirming what Schopenhauer suspected: the past exists alongside the present and the future as a place, not a period of time.

We are adrift in a world that seems scarcely comprehensible, one in which old borders disappear in a flash, and, just as quickly, new borders are declared. We require for our rescue, as is so often true, a tool that does not now exist: an imaginary atlas.

Such an atlas would map the borders of the world, natural and humanly imposed, in all their multitude. It would be an unseemly clutter of names and symbols, for while there are few sacred places left, there is iconography in abundance, as though someone had called out, "Grant us a sign, O Lord!" and God had responded, by cruel custom, literally: "Don't touch the merchandise." "We aim to please. You aim too, please." *"Massima velocità 120."* *"Cede la luz."* This is not so bad, for clutter is part of modern life, as everyone knows who has seen an empty lot sprout a shopping complex overnight, and as the melancholy Joseph Conrad, who had everywhere seen the destruction of the natural world for the imposition of a new and inferior one, observed a century ago in *Heart of Darkness*:

> [Africa] was not a blank space any more. It had got filled since my boyhood with rivers and lakes and names. It had ceased to be a blank space of delightful mystery—a white patch for a boy to dream gloriously over. It had become a place of darkness.

An epistemological paradox: things become dark as we come to know them, the darkness of type on a map, of meridians inscribed and projections drawn. And how much we have to know. Ecologists tell us that the first step to geographic understanding is the ability to describe one's own place. Peter Warshall, an expert on watersheds and arid-lands ecosystems, defines this more closely by asking us to describe, at this moment, the soil series on which we are standing. The poet Gary Snyder, who locates the gods in such things, suggests that we have not inhabited a place until we can name at least a hundred species of flora and fauna—more information that would have to be packed in our rapidly expanding, even overflowing atlas, dark with multicolored inks.

We would want to know the ancient names of all places, for the past is a land we may inhabit whenever we wish. What did the Homeric poets and wild

Germanic hunters and Carthaginian merchants call Marseilles and the horsy marshes of Provence? By what names did the Kwakiutl Indians call Seattle and the Strait of Juan de Fuca? And the conflicting names: what did the Akimel O'odham, Tohono O'odham, and San Carlos Apache variously call Tucson—and why did none of them prevail? How did the Alaskan *Denali* come finally to replace the American *Mount McKinley*? Why and how were Soviet and Eastern European place-names bearing reference to Josef Stalin and Leonid Brezhnev so quickly rechristened in the last quarter of the twentieth century? We would want to redress thousands of instances of *damnatio memoriae* from the past.

We would seek to discover the nature of indigenous, prescientific geographical knowledge in the world. Did the Ioway know that far to their south lay a great body of water, as the Dieguéños of the southern California coast knew that off to the east lay vast deserts and huge mountain chains? Native conceptions of place, of the otherworld, of spatial relationships would quickly fill the infinite pages of our infinite, Borgesian book. Our atlas would sing the songlines of the indigenous Australians, the network of chants with which, Bruce Chatwin has conjectured, our nomadic ancestors encircled the globe, calling the world and human consciousness into being, naming and remembering each detail of the land by the totemic objects and animals inhabiting it. It would re-create the great cadastral surveys of the Incas and the Aztecs, the sailing charts of the ancient Polynesians as they made their way over the islands to Tahiti and Rapa Nui, to America. It would recover the poetry that the modern world has buried.

In our atlas, the sand-ringed bays of Palestine—a name competing with so many others through history that the pages devoted to it would soon grow impossibly dark—would have names in Phoenician, Assyrian, Hittite, Lycian, Lydian, Greek, Latin, Bulgarian, Arabic, Old French, Ladino, Spanish, Maltese, Egyptian, and a dozen other languages. The grim new cities of Siberia would resound with Chukchee and Turkic alongside Russian words, of the Brazilian interior with Kalapalo and Bororo and Gê alongside the resonant Portuguese of the conquerors. Etymologies would surround every place on our darkening map: the reader would know that *Mexico* comes from the Nahuatl meaning "navel in the center of the lake of the moon," that *China* is a corruption of *Chung Kuo*, "the Middle Kingdom," and that Fruitland, Utah, not far from Mount Carmel, was known to early Anglo settlers as Rabbit Gulch but renamed by developers to lure unsuspecting investors to a dry and unforgiving region.

An imaginary atlas would, naturally enough, embrace the imagined. In the 1950s, infinitesimal portions of Alaskan land were offered as a premium to promote a brand of cereal. We would want to draw our map of that place to reflect those thousands of tiny parcels, to show the bilked their worthless deeds to the soil of Mars. We would not wish to forget the fabulous lands of Gaius Julius Solinus's *Polyhistor,* where centaurs with elephantine ears canter over the earth and vipers urinate amber and other precious stones, nor to overlook the legends of the hyperborean kingdom of Prester John and the Isles of the Blessed—or even the lost continent of Atlantis, which has so exercised the charlatan imagination for centuries. We would want to locate the Seven Cities of Cibola, Shangri-La, the Antarctic of Edgar Poe's *The Narrative of Arthur Gordon Pym,* Abbott's mysterious Flatland, all evasions from the world around us, the world of towering mountains, sweeping plains, glittering estuaries, and jagged escarpments.

We would not discount the mad claims of the new conquistadors, such as the American businessmen who in 1972 declared a pile of volcanic cinders hundreds of miles south of Tonga to be "the Republic of Minerva," a tax-free *paradiso terrestrialis,* or Leicester Hemingway, brother of Ernest, who in 1964 installed himself as the ruler of New Atlantis, a raft off the coast of Jamaica, long since destroyed by the tides.

The imaginary atlas would entertain dreams: the afterworld of the Ghost Dancers, the stateless nations of the Armenians, the Kurds, the Mashpee Indians of New England, the Sikhs of northern India, and a million forgotten wishes for sovereignty and self-determination. It would ceaselessly question the past, the real and the imagined, and it would interrogate the future: How will the exploration and colonization of space affect the naming of cities in the years to come? In what language will the cities that will one day line the ocean floor be named?

Such an atlas is possible, thanks to computers and the arcane mathematics of fractal geometry, whereby the hitherto unmappable, minute variations in landforms can now be drawn and replicated. Somewhere all the necessary data exist or can be inferred. But our infinite, all-embracing text will likely never come to be. For real atlases are political artifacts, representing convenient fractions of what we know and can know about the world. Brazilian atlases place the Americas in the center of the world, just as Japanese atlases place Japan and French atlases place France at the axis of the globe. Atlases manufactured in the United States still often do not call Cambodia by its indigenous name, Kampuchea, or set *Ho Chi Minh City* outside of the parentheses that *Saigon* now must inhabit.

The world assumes alien shapes invented only by power. Things become dark as we know them. That darkness is variable. We can, if we wish, know that in middle America there lies a belt of signs reading "Take all you want, but eat all you take" and "Get US out of UN," that in the Mexican republic a menacing curtain means to separate *jipis* from the rest of the world. The future is unwritten, the imaginable lies everywhere before us. There are places on earth that seem to give up their secrets as readily as do gossiping teenagers, and then there are others—mountain summits, riverine canyons, rain forests, deserts, the floors of silent seas—that were once privileged to stand as mysteries. Nothing now is off-limits. There is no longer terra incognita. The darkness grows.

But we can direct where the shadow falls. "God," wrote the Catalan theologian Alain Llull in the twelfth century, borrowing in turn from the third-century *Gnostic Corpus Hermeticum,* "is an intelligible sphere whose center is everywhere and whose circumference is nowhere."

In other words, as the modern Gaian ecology of the British scientist James Lovelock proclaims, God is the world, and the world is God. The imaginary atlas seeks to locate the divinity. We have not yet begun to catalog God's nine billion names in all that we have lost.

The Unknowable Wild

Kamchatka. For hours I have been traveling with the arc of the sun, crossing time zones and continents, flying the great circle from Los Angeles to Shanghai. Between those two huge megalopolises, far below, has passed territory that a Puritan elder, one of those dour thinkers who first shaped—and who continue to shape—American ideas about wilderness, would call a hellish wasteland: the glacial inlets of British Columbia, the old-growth forests of the Alaskan coast, the tundra of Beringia. And now Kamchatka, a place of childhood dreams nursed by an often visited globe and by peripatetic parents, Kamchatka, wilderness pure and primeval, uncut by roads, seemingly unvisited, a russet forested world stretching unbroken from horizon to horizon.

Just weeks before I had been in another wilderness, the Yaak Valley of northwestern Montana, tucked away near the Idaho and British Columbia lines. It is but an atom of wild land compared to the huge landmass of the Kamchatka Peninsula, but it is surpassingly wild nonetheless, a place where wildlife corridors do not run at right angles, a place through which a Yellowstone-bound wolf might find safe passage on the underground railroad from Canada. Small it may be, but it is largely unmediated by human presence.

I had traveled to nearby Troy, Montana, to provide desperately needed moral guidance to a cutthroat gang of musicians who were then touring taverns and trailer parks in the northwestern corner of the state, but Yaak was the real reason I had traveled so far from home—Yaak, about which I had been reading for so many years in the journalism and essays of my friend Rick Bass. Rick is not shy about sharing Yaak, while I selfishly salt away my favorite places, the little wild corners of Arizona, New Mexico, Sonora. And so on a sweltering July day we set out from the banks of the Yaak River up a spiny knoll in the all too evident footsteps of an adolescent male grizzly bear—I say that he was male and adolescent on account of the hormone-charged trail of savaged tree trunks and half-chewed shrubs he had left in his wake, but I have no stronger evidence for his identity—through a tangled association of coral root, tallgrass, mistletoe, blackberry, lodgepole pine, spruce, alder, cedar, ponderosa pine, an Amazonian density of vegetation bewildering to me, used to the comparative austerity of the Sonoran Desert.

We never did catch up with that bear, although I like to believe with more hope than proof that we saw the barest flash of his tail rounding a draw a quarter of a mile or so ahead of us. The grizzly surely knew we were in pursuit. It is probably to the good that we did not meet him. It is certainly to the good that he had a place in this world big enough that he could afford to tolerate our attentions.

"Among the most sinister phenomena in intellectual history is the avoidance of the concrete," says one of my great heroes, the philosopher Elias Canetti. Traveling into Yaak—and, for that matter, flying over the reddish eternity of Kamchatka and Siberia—gave mere abstractions about which I had read in books and on maps an unforgettable face. Portions have been ravaged over time, to be sure, but Yaak is one of the few wild places, few *real* places, left in the contiguous United States. It is a place where the processes of nature—growth and decline, decay and regeneration, birth and death—are laid bare before us. Having now gazed into its face, I am even more firmly convinced of its value, and of its being precisely the sort of place that demands our protection—against logging, mining, ranching, and other activities that favor short-term gain over long-term good.

We have too few such places. It is time, now and finally, to declare that what we have we will for once not allow to be taken from us.

I have been thinking about places like Yaak for years, and that thinking came about by one of those accidental remarks that can forever change lives.

Many years ago, on a train crossing the coastal plain of southern Italy, I fell into conversation with an Englishman about my age who, he was quick to tell me, had just earned a sizable fortune by buying old dockside warehouses in London and selling them as luxury apartments to people who had been busily earning sizable fortunes of their own. He asked where I was from. When I told him Arizona, he smiled and said, "I've been there, once. Quite a beautiful place, really. All that extraordinary land, but"—here he paused meaningfully—"there's nothing on it."

Well, I replied, gazing out at the snarled macchia and tangled drifts of prickly Apulian cactus, by my lights you're off by a word in the chain of cause and effect: all that beautiful land, *and* there's nothing on it.

The Englishman's attitude, neither benign nor malignant, was not at all surprising. The received European vision of the land differs markedly from our own: it defines the natural environment, nostalgically, as a collection of not only forests, rivers, and mountains but also thatch-roofed farmhouses in sylvan glens, a curl of smoke rising from the chimneys and lambs bleating in clovery meadows full of swarming bees, fair-haired children dancing around a maypole and strong elders smoking their meerschaums. I am exaggerating that Tolkienesque vision, but not by much, and lately I have been struck by how often it occurs in European nature writing. A land without people, in much of that library, is no land at all.

There can be little or no unmanaged nature in such a conception of the land, and for good reason: only in lesser-visited corners of highland Scotland and pockets of the Balkans, among a few other places, has Europe left much of its land alone. "It is difficult," the Dutch historian Simon Schama writes in *Landscape and Memory*, "to think of a single natural system that has not, for better or worse, been substantially modified by human culture." Difficult for a European observer such as my Isle of Dogs conversant, perhaps, but not difficult at all from where I sit as I write these words, looking out at tall mountains that are pockmarked by evidence of human enterprise, to be sure, yet far from substantially changed, still harboring black bears and cougars, ringtails and bighorn sheep, still indifferent to our doings.

That bar-car conversation took place in less chewed-up times. The desert had not yet begun to teem with trailer parks and regional metrocenters, with convenience markets and, improbably, tree-lined lakes ringed by condominiums. Neither did Beijing have a subway, London a Hard Rock Cafe. The solitude of places that have not been severely modified by us busy humans is still close at hand in Arizona—and in just about every other state, even urbanized Rhode Island—for those who take a moment to find it. But that solitude, here and everywhere, is being lost daily, and there is much to be done if it is not to disappear entirely, its loss marked by days on a calendar page.

By now it is a commonplace among environmentalists to say that we need more wilderness. Indeed we do. It is unreasonable, I think, to suggest otherwise—only a few developers, who form the single most powerful political lobby in America, stand to benefit from the destruction of wild places—and it heartens me to see proposals afloat like that of the Wildlands Project, which aims to link undeveloped areas of North America with easements to allow wildlife safe passage from place to place, and that of the Utah Wilderness Coalition, whose projected amalgamation of wild lands around the Golden Circle of national parks holds the promise of making a vast natural protectorate that would dwarf several European countries. To tender such proposals in these boom-and-bust, go-go-go days is not easy; whereas, for instance, the Utah Wilderness Coalition had been petitioning Congress for an area of at least 5 million acres to set aside from development, Utah's congressional delegation offered only 1.8 million acres—still a vast parcel of territory, but nowhere near big enough for the job at hand. President Clinton's designation, in 1996, of some of those lands as the Escalante Wilderness is just a start.

That job is to preserve something of the American wild as it existed at the time of the first human arrival, to keep safe that fine corner of the world that a

Puritan leader indeed once characterized as a "savage, howling waste of wolves." The biologist E. O. Wilson has noted that the number of plant and animal species doubles with every tenfold increase in area, and, while remarking that "wilderness has virtue unto itself and needs no extraneous justification," he suggests that it is a matter of enlightened self-interest—extraneous justification of immediate power—to allow that wilderness to prevail. Who knows the potential, for instance, of a new pharmacopoeia derived from plants that are not yet known or studied, the insights into our own beings that might come from observing life not under our dominion? If you set aside a postage stamp of land you may spare some rare mycorrhiza (the Yaak, for example, harbors a fungus that has symbiotic value for the Pacific yew tree, from which, in turn, is derived the cancer-impeding drug Taxol). Set aside a large piece of territory, however, and you create an evolutionary laboratory, less a museum, as cynics have suggested, than a savings bank with a rate of return that can never quite be calculated.

More wilderness is wanted, yes—or, better, less human involvement with lands already wholly or partially wild. But with the mere fact of more land, mere numbers in a preservationist's inventory, we need to rethink wilderness in the political discussions that have been forming around it so that wilderness is more than just a slogan, what William Hazlitt called "the most airy abstraction," a sinister avoidance of the kind against which Elias Canetti so rightly warned. Wilderness is a place, of course, a tangible thing. It is *real.* It is also a governing idea in the way we perceive ourselves as Americans, an idea that finds expression in a recent *New York Times* survey, eight in ten of whose respondents considered themselves to be environmentalists, in favor of substantially more government protection of what wild land remains within our borders.

That is good news indeed for friends of wilderness, who have been having a hard time of it on Capitol Hill over the last few years, but who will, I think, ultimately prevail, thanks to friends like Bruce Vento, a Democratic representative from Minnesota who in 1994 wisely warned a gathering of environmentalists, in the language of business, "If you write off Congress, the degradation of existing laws and the defeat of new proposals for environmental protection will become a self-fulfilling prophecy. Remember, the public is with you. Wilderness is a product that the American people like."

Yes, it is, although I dislike thinking of wilderness as a "product." Thanks to our fondness for it, Americans enjoy more real wilderness than do the citizens of most other countries. That may not always be the case, given how rapidly our wilderness is disappearing; it may be that one day wilderness is little more than a cherished concept, a tenet of official mythology that will remain when, as Henry Thoreau remarked a century and a half ago, "American liberty is a thing of the past."

A wilderness is fundamentally, as in the Anglo-Saxon, a *wild-deor-ness*, a place of "wild animalness," the domain of creatures other than humans; as my friend Doug Peacock has observed, "It isn't wilderness unless something in it can kill you and eat you." (The Irish poet Brendan Behan rejoins, "If God hadn't meant for us to be eaten, he wouldn't have made us of meat.") The operative notion here is that of a fastness in which humans, or at least human societies, have no dominant place. The operative laws are those of nature, of systole and diastole, ebb and flow, birth and death, the order that the singer of Ecclesiastes knew so well.

That wilderness is a place where a falling tree will make a mighty crash indeed without our being there to hear it. I do not begrudge people their sojourns in such places, their residences on the edges, but I would just as soon see wilderness retain its native meaning as the sole domain of wild animals, largely innocent of human encounters. This may seem a curious attitude, and I have more than once been taken to task for airing it. "How can you be a nature writer," an exasperated gentleman once asked me at a writers' conference, "without being *in* nature?"

My reply was then and is now that nature, like the kingdom of heaven, is all around us and within us— especially, I might add, in places with much wild land, places like Arizona and Montana. We need not run with the wolves or dance with the bears to content ourselves with the notion that there are properly worlds that are not ours to comprehend. It is enough, in my estimation, merely to know that such worlds exist. We have overrun quite enough territory as it is. We can, and we must, leave what remains alone.

In his ethnographic memoir *Tristes Tropiques* the French anthropologist Claude Lévi-Strauss remarks that pretechnological societies begin to unravel the moment an anthropologist or missionary sets foot in their longhouses or wikiups. So, too, I fear, do orders of nature sometimes begin to dissolve the minute a Vibram-soled boot crushes a figwort. I want at least some country about which cartographers can write, as their medieval peers did, only the words, "Beyond here lie dragons." I want places in which the historian who called American history one continuous real-estate transaction would for once be proven wrong. I want places where nature knows humans not, or only a little.

I know a few such places. I am happy not to visit them again, to let them go about their ancient business without me. In one, the Gila Wilderness of New Mexico, the oldest federally designated wilderness area in the nation, I once spent a full-moon vigil across a glade from a female mountain lion who studied me with casual indifference, yawning repeatedly to air her lack of concern that I had invaded her place. In another, the Swansea Wilderness of western Arizona, on a fine, warm late-March evening, my only company was a curious kit fox who scampered into my campsite to examine the unaccustomed light of my campfire. He did not know enough to mistrust humans, and I still feel pangs of shame for having disturbed his solitude. In still another, the Yaak, that storied and heartachingly beautiful place, I experienced the next best thing to seeing a grizzly bear in the wild—and that is not seeing a grizzly on its home turf while knowing that he was there, waiting, just over the next rise. I do not have to go there again. The bear can do just fine without me.

I want to know that many more such places exist, that we still live in a world that can imaginatively accommodate this unknowable wild, just as that Yaak grizzly once accommodated a tourist from far away. "The great vice of Americans," the English poet W. H. Auden once observed, "is not materialism but a lack of respect for matter." Working together for more wilderness, I think we are coming to respect matter a great deal more than we ever have. Working to save Yaak—and Kamchatka, and Siberia, and the Mogollon Rim, and all the other wild places that are left to us—will yield our own earthly salvation. In that dawning respect and recognition lies our true geography of hope: the preservation of vast, unquantifiable, unknowable sweeps of beautiful land—*and* with nothing on it.

Walking

Solvitur ambulando, Saint Jerome was fond of saying. To solve a problem, walk around. Walk until your shoe leather falls off, until no moleskin patch in the world can save the tattered remnants of your heels—only walk, walk as only a human can until the mysteries of the ages unravel before you.

Jerome had grand ambitions: to convert the world to a rising faith. Mine have always been smaller: to get a handle on whatever happens to be on my mind at a given time, to wrestle a few problems to the ground. I have solved a few of them—but probably not enough—by following his advice. I have roamed across alpine meanders in Germany, blithely enjoying the Wanderjahre of youth while my soldier father awaited the seemingly imminent Soviet attack on the Fulda Gap. I have walked, over the years, down much of the length of the Appalachian Trail, dodging black bears and eighteen-wheelers alike in that battleground of city and country; over desert paths on the coast of Baja California, once isolated but now clogged with resort hotels; along soggy byways through Somerset and Cornwall, where something of an older Europe endures; across windswept dune-fields on the Icelandic coast, a landscape that makes it clear why those old Norse myths are both so noble and so terrifying.

When I was a university student in the mid-1970s, I worked over two summers as an archaeological assistant in southern Italy. The small town in which I lived had been noted in antiquity both as the birthplace of the poet Horace and as a pleasant stopover along the Appian Way, the object of our survey; its last claim to fame was as the birthplace of one of Mussolini's field marshalls. Afterward the town had languished, just another whitewashed village in the shadow of the Apennine Mountains, no place for sophisticates. The town was poor, so poor that the residents of nearby towns called their neighbors *indiani*, as if they were a slice of Calcutta transplanted to Europe. For all its poverty it seemed joyful, however, an apparent contradiction that I pondered on many walks through its streets.

The landscape was littered with trails: goatpaths that had been in use since the Neolithic era; footpaths from Roman times, still carefully maintained so that the locals, accustomed to the ebb and flow of European history, could make for the hills at a moment's notice; cobbled lanes that led to lush vineyards, plum orchards, and olive groves; and far on the flatlands below, a modern *autostrada* that spread its black band of asphalt from Milan to the heel of Italy. Aside from the last intrusion, it was all a walker's dream. Indeed, the people of the village, like most rural Mediterraneans, practiced the custom of ambling each fair-weather evening in a continuous loop through the town, a *passeggiatta* that allowed everyone the chance to visit, if only for a moment, with their neighbors. (Were Americans to take up this custom, the rate of criminal violence would surely drop, for it's easier to gun down strangers than people with whom you've passed the time.)

Walking, I learned over those summers, helps sharpen the senses. At a Pleistocene gait, far removed from the jet airliners and fast auto engines that blur our vision of the world, the walker makes out the shapes of things, learns to distinguish the differences between look-alike plants, to separate out the churring of myriad insects and the whirring of birds—and even to solve a few puzzles. Sometimes the pedestrian's senses can even become too sharp. One early morning while walking among olive orchards that lined a small river, I had the strange perception that I could see straight through the now-shaking trees, that their atoms had somehow disincorporated or that I had suddenly attained X-ray vision like Superman. A few seconds passed until I noticed that the ground below me had momentarily become rubbery. Only then did I realize that I was witnessing an earthquake, that my small corner of the world had indeed flown apart for an instant.

Much of the walking I did in southern Italy was far less revealing. My daily work involved lugging a theodolite across newly plowed fields, hopping among clods of dirt two feet across. The deep plows turned up soil two meters deep, so that buried artifacts from ancient times—bits of pottery or tile, say, or the occasional piece of lead pipe—would be dredged up to the surface. Whenever our team encountered a scatter of such artifacts, we would measure the area, plot it on Italian artillery maps of only nodding accuracy, and then move on in search of the next scatter. It was exhausting work, more suited to oxen than to humans; even the farmers avoided walking in those churned-up fields. In two summers, by my estimate, we traversed twelve hundred miles of black soil, a part of Italy that very few visitors ever see, or would ever want to see.

I solved a career problem in walking those fields. Walkers cannot help but think, after all, if only to distract from sore backs and aching feet. I decided that the glamorous world of archaeology was not to be my profession; the slogging was just too hard. Instead, I became an editor, and then a writer, making a run for unplowed hills whenever the wanderlust became too much to handle.

Nearly two decades later, I find myself spending long stretches of time roaming the deserts and mountains of the Southwest. To live in the desert requires a certain kind of madness—that specific disease of dogs and the English—that is epidemic out this way. To wander off into that desert, alone or in company, is to test the very limits of one's endurance and to tempt the end of one's tenure on this otherwise green planet.

Such ventures make us human. Or, better: it is the walking itself that makes us human, that defines our nature. Our ability to raise ourselves on two feet and not fall over while moving distinguishes us from all other animal species. Only as a consequence of that ability could our brain cases expand enough to allow us to hold the thoughts we have since had, for good or ill. Only then did our laryngeal tract, tugged downward thanks to our newly erect posture, expand so that we could form speech. Thus most babies walk before they talk, and stop crying when they are rocked back and forth, a rhythm that emulates walking.

We were made to wander afoot—read Roy Lewis's subtly hilarious novel *The Evolution Man* for the evidence—and we were made to keep moving. When we settle down, it seems, we tend as a species to become nastier rather than more civilized: the Mongol hordes notwithstanding, nomadic peoples do not loll about inventing secret-police organizations, atomic weapons, and taxes.

Idle feet, it turns out, are the devil's real workshop.

Solvitur ambulando. It is solved by walking around. Walk on quietly, for, as the peripatetic American poet Marianne Moore once observed, "The deepest feeling always shows itself in silence."

Just walk on.

About the Author

Gregory McNamee is the author or editor of seventeen books, among them *The Mountain World: A Literary Journey* (Sierra Club Books, 2000), *Grand Canyon Place Names* (The Mountaineers, 1997), and *Gila: The Life and Death of an American River* (Crown Publishers, 1994/University of New Mexico Press, 1998). He is also the author of the texts for two books of photographs, *In the Presence of Wolves* (with Art Wolfe, Crown Publishers, 1995) and *Open Range & Parking Lots* (with Virgil Hancock, University of New Mexico Press, 1999).

McNamee is a former correspondent for *Outside,* a columnist for *New Times,* a contributing editor for *The Bloomsbury Review,* and a regular contributor to many other periodicals. More than two thousand of his articles, essays, short stories, poems, and translations have appeared in the United States and abroad. He is also a contributing editor for Amazon.com, writing regularly on nature and ecology, science, technology, world history, and music.

McNamee lives in Tucson, Arizona, where he works as a writer, journalist, and editor.